ENTREPRENEURSHIP

edited by

STUART BRUCHEY
UNIVERSITY OF MAINE

A GARLAND SERIES

AFRICAN-AMERICAN ECONOMIC DEVELOPMENT AND SMALL BUSINESS OWNERSHIP

KILOLO KIJAKAZI

GARLAND PUBLISHING, Inc.
New York & London / 1997

Library of Congress Cataloging-in-Publication Data

Kijakazi, Kilolo.
    African-American economic development and small business
ownership / Kilolo Kijakazi.
            p.   cm. — (Garland studies in entrepreneurship)
        Includes bibliographical references and index.
        ISBN 0-8153-2999-7 (alk. paper)
        1. Afro-American business enterprises—History. 2. Afro-
Americans—Economic conditions. 3. Afro-Americans—Social
conditions. I. Title. II. Series.
HD2346.U5K54 1997
338.6'422'08996073—dc21

                                                        97-23244

Printed on acid-free, 250-year-life paper
Manufactured in the United States of America

To my family,
who supported me,
my friends,
who encouraged me,
and the African-American community,
which inspired me.

Contents

List of Tables   *ix*

Preface   *xiii*

Introduction   *xv*

List of Abbreviations   *xix*

I. Background   3
    Economic Development and Business Ownership   5
    Historical Perspective   5
    Reasons for Limited Presence of African-
       American Firms   16

II. Economic Development Models and Legislation   21
    Alternative Proposals for Economic Development   21
    Current Policies and Programs   27
    Assessment of Current Policies and Programs   31
    Recent Legislative and Judicial Actions   33

III. Research on African-American Business Ownership   39
    Previous Research   39
    Limitations of Previous Research   45
    Expansion on Previous Research   49

IV. Methodology   51

Overview   51
Research Questions   52
Target Population   52
Data Source   53
Data Analysis   53

V. Analysis of the Data   61
Results   61
Discussion   78

VI. Policy Recommendations   89
Start-Up Capital   89
College Education   93
Managerial Experience   100
Policy Recommendations Concerning Other Variables
      in the Model   101
Microenterprise for Low-Income Entrepreneurs   102
Block Grants   103
Summary   104

Appendix A   107

Appendix B   111

Appendix C   115

Bibliography   121

Index   133

Tables

1. Univariate Analysis of African-American Sample, with
   All Respondents for Professional Services, FIRE,
   Wholesale and Manufacturing Industries Combined   62

2. Univariate Analysis of African-American Logistic
   Sample for Professional Services, FIRE,
   Wholesale, and Manufacturing Industries Combined   63

3. Univariate Analysis of Nonminority-Male Sample, with
   All Respondents for Professional Services, FIRE,
   Wholesale, and Manufacturing Industries Combined   65

4. Univariate Analysis of Nonminority-Male Logistic
   Sample for Professional Services, FIRE,
   Wholesale, and Manufacturing Industries Combined   66

5. Real Gross Domestic Product by Industry as a Percentage
   of Real Gross Domestic Product, 1987 and 1991   67

6. Distribution of Firms by Race and Industry   68

7. Multiple Logistic Regression Analysis of African-American
   Firms in Wholesale and Manufacturing Industries
   Combined   71

8. Multiple Logistic Regression Analysis of Nonminority-Male Firms in Wholesale and Manufacturing Industries Combined   72

9. Multiple Logistic Regression Analysis of African-American Firms in Professional Services and FIRE Industries Combined   73

10. Multiple Logistic Regression Analysis of Nonminority-Male Firms in Professional Services and FIRE Industries Combined   75

11. Multiple Logistic Regression Analysis of African-American Firms in Wholesale and Manufacturing Industries Combined, with Growth in State Employment   76

12. Multiple Logistic Regression Analysis of Nonminority-Male Firms in Wholesale and Manufacturing Industries Combined, with Growth in State Employment   77

13. Multiple Logistic Regression Analysis of African-American Firms in Professional Services and FIRE Industries Combined, with Growth in State Employment   79

14. Multiple Logistic Regression Analysis of Nonminority-Male Firms in Professional Services and FIRE Industries Combined, with Growth in State Employment   80

15. Multiple Logistic Regression Analysis of African-American Firms, Comparing Professional Services and FIRE Industries Combined with Wholesale and Manufacturing Industries Combined   81

16. Multiple Logistic Regression Analysis of Nonminority-Male Firms, Comparing Professional Services and FIRE Industries Combined with Wholesale and Manufacturing Industries Combined   82

17. Percent of Firms Having Owners with College Degrees,
 by Race and Industry   84

B1. Bivariate Logistic Regression Analysis of African-American
 Firms in Professional Services, FIRE, Wholesale, and
 Manufacturing Industries Combined   112

B2. Bivariate Logistic Regression Analysis of Nonminority-Male
 Firms in Professional Services, FIRE, Wholesale, and
 Manufacturing Industries Combined   113

C1. Multiple Logistic Regression Analysis of African-American
 Firms in the Professional Services Industry   116

C2. Multiple Logistic Regression Analysis of Nonminority-Male
 Firms in the Professional Services Industry   117

C3. Multiple Logistic Regression Analysis of African-American
 Firms in the FIRE Industry   118

C4. Multiple Logistic Regression Analysis of Nonminority-Male
 Firms in the FIRE Industry   119

C5. Multiple Logistic Regression Analysis of African-American
 Firms in the Wholesale Industry   120

C6. Multiple Logistic Regression Analysis of Nonminority-Male
 Firms in the Wholesale Industry   121

C7. Multiple Logistic Regression Analysis of African-American
 Firms in the Manufacturing Industry   123

C8. Multiple Logistic Regression Analysis of Nonminority-Male
 Firms in the Manufacturing Industry   124

Preface

This book examines the history of economic development in the African-American community and the use of entrepreneurship to improve the economic well-being of its members. African-Americans have engaged in entrepreneurship for as long as they have been in America. Business ownership has also been advanced by policy makers for over 25 years to address the economic status of this community. Given the importance placed on business ownership, it is essential to understand the factors that affect the success of small, African-American firms in order to effectively shape public policy.

Previous studies have examined such factors and found that the initial financial capital investment, or start-up capital, is an important determinant of success. The limitation of these studies is that they analyzed African-American businesses in the aggregate. The research in this book improves on previous studies by analyzing factors related to business success by industry and region. The primary research question is whether start-up capital, education, and managerial experience are significantly related to the survival of African-American firms when businesses are disaggregated by industry and region. Four industry groups were examined, including professional services; finance, insurance, and real estate; manufacturing; and wholesale trade. The data were also disaggregated by state to determine whether local economic factors were associated with success.

The primary source of data used for this study was the 1987 Characteristics of Business Owners database compiled by the U.S. Bureau of the Census. Logistic regression analysis was used to identify the factors associated with business viability. Based on the results of this analysis, a set of policy recommendations was developed to facilitate entrepreneurship for African Americans.

Introduction

The first objective of this research is to examine African-American small business ownership as a vehicle for improving the economic well-being of the African-American community. The second is to determine how public policy can be shaped to 1) prepare African Americans for entrepreneurship, 2) facilitate their entry into business, and 3) improve the odds for the success of these small businesses, resulting in a net gain in the number of such firms.

Clearly, the economic status of African Americans continues to lag behind that of whites. After many years of progress for African Americans, the disparity between the two groups appears to be widening. The recent policy debate involving Congress and the White House has resulted in legislation which may create further economic uncertainty for African Americans across a broad range of income levels. Efforts to reduce the size of government may mean a substantial loss of jobs for the middle and working class. As African Americans are disproportionately employed in the public sector, they are consequently vulnerable to plans to downsize government (Green & Pryde, 1989). Those employed in the private as well as public sector may face fewer opportunities for job promotion, in light of actions which may eliminate or limit provisions of affirmative action. New entrants to the job market may have increased difficulty obtaining a job.

Low-income families are facing the consequences of the new Personal Responsibility and Work Opportunity Act, passed in August of 1996. This law eliminated the Aid to Families with Dependent Children public assistance program and replaced it, along with emergency assistance and work programs, with block grants to states. This new program of block grants is called Temporary Assistance for Needy Families (TANF) and has minimal federal requirements as to how states should spend the money.

States were given increased flexibility in designing and administering public assistance; however, the amount of funds they will receive in their block grants each year will be fixed, regardless of changes in economic conditions. For the first time since 1935, low-income families will not be guaranteed public assistance. Not only can states change the rules for determining who is eligible for TANF, no family can receive benefits for more than a total of five years over their lifetime.

The new welfare reform law also substantially changed the Food Stamp Program. Nearly $28 million will be cut from this program's budget between 1996 and 2002. In addition, able-bodied adults who are not raising children will be limited to only three months of benefits out of every three years, unless they are working at least 20 hours a week or participating in a work program.

What is needed is a means by which African Americans can secure their economic well-being. The current congressional and executive branches of government have placed great emphasis on self-sufficiency. Yet, they have paid little attention to the development of an economy that can sustain these legislative changes. Self-sufficiency requires an adequate number of jobs for those who need them. These jobs must pay enough to remove people from poverty and must be stable enough to provide long-term economic security. If an insufficient number of jobs exists, then job creation is necessary.

Beyond job creation, economically distressed communities require increasing inflows of resources. An increasing tax base is also needed to allow these communities to improve services, public institutions, and infrastructures for residents.

Entrepreneurship is one means by which African Americans can create jobs for themselves, hire other African Americans, and increase revenues for their communities. Entrepreneurship is not a new idea; for over 25 years, policy makers at the federal, state, and local levels of government have proposed business ownership as a means of improving the economic status of African Americans. These proposals have not always been based on a clear understanding of the African-American experience with regard to economic development, nor of what factors are crucial to the viability of African-American businesses.

This book breaks new ground by taking a comprehensive look at African-American economic development and at how business ownership fits into this development. First, it defines economic development and describes its link to entrepreneurship (Chapter I). While a great deal has been written about the uses of entrepreneurship as a means of economic development, the rationale for the assumption that entrepreneurship will lead to economic development has rarely been explained.

Next, this study uses qualitative and quantitative research to examine entrepreneurship. The qualitative research highlights some early research on African-American economic development and business enterprise that has all too frequently been overlooked by others. For instance, researchers who have made cross-cultural comparisons of entrepreneurship in America have, for the most part, concluded that African Americans, unlike Asian Americans and Jewish Americans, do not have a tradition of entrepreneurship. This study provides an extensive history of the actions of African Americans to secure their economic independence, including business creation. Furthermore, this study describes the traditions from African economic systems which African Americans perpetuated during and after slavery and used to create their own institutions and enterprises.

This book also contains a review of some of the major policy initiatives undertaken and laws passed to promote African-American business ownership (Chapter II). In light of the number of actions taken by policy makers since the 1960s, it is important to understand what has already been done in order to assess what may be needed in the future. Therefore, this work examines previous research on African-American business ownership (Chapter III).

These other studies found considerable variation in the viability of African-American firms. They also examined the factors associated with business viability. However, the key limitation of this previous research is that, for the most part, it analyzed African-American firms in the aggregate. The conclusions reached about these firms as a whole are not necessarily true for the subparts. This book addresses the limitations of previous research via quantitative analyses.

These quantitative analyses contribute to knowledge by determining the factors related to the survival of African-American businesses by industry (Chapters IV and V). The nationwide 1987 Characteristics of Business Owners database was analyzed using logistic regression models to examine African-American firms in the emerging fields of professional services; finance, insurance, and real estate; wholesale and manufacturing. This database contains information on both the firms and their owners. It is a much richer and more recent source of information than has been used by many other researchers. Consequently, a more rigorous analysis was possible.

Finally, this book sets forth for policy makers recommendations soundly based on a comprehensive understanding of the history and dynamics of African-American enterprise (Chapter VI). These recommendations are not constrained by the current political environment. Rather, they flow from the qualitative and quantitative findings of this research.

List of Abbreviations

ACE	American Council on Education
CORE	Congress on Racial Equality
CBO	Characteristics of Business Owners
CDC	Community development corporation
CDFI	Community Development Financial Institution
CRA	Community Reinvestment Act
DHHS	U.S. Department of Health and Human Services
DOT	Department of Transportation
EOL	Equal Opportunity Loan Program
FCC	Federal Communications Commission
FDIC	Federal Deposit Insurance Corporation
FIRE	Finance, insurance, and real estate
FNMA	Federal National Mortgage Association
GNP	Gross National Product
HBCU	Historically Black Colleges and Universities
HUD	U.S. Department of Housing and Urban Development
IRS	U.S. Internal Revenue Service
M	Mean (arithmetic average)
MBDA	Minority Business Development Agency
MBDC	Minority Business Development Centers
Mdn	Median
N	Total number in the sample
OSDBU	Office of Small Disadvantaged Business Utilization
p	Probability
Q	Quartile
Q3-Q1	Interquartile range
SBA	Small Business Association
SBIC	Small Business Investment Company

SD	Standard deviation
SIC	Standard Industrial Classification
SMSA	Standard Metropolitan Statistical Area
SSBIC	Specialized Small Business Investment Companies
TANF	Temporary Assistance to Needy Families
USDA	U.S. Department of Agriculture
X^2	Chi Square

African-American
Economic Development and
Small Business Ownership

I
Background

In 1989, the National Research Council of the National Academy of Sciences released a report on the economic status of African Americans (Jaynes & Williams, Jr., 1989). The Council concluded that, according to several indicators, the economic gap between African Americans and whites might well be growing. It further stated that the economic advancement which had begun in 1940 had been arrested over the past two decades. Factors contributing to this slowdown in economic growth were racial discrimination and recessions in the national economy. The Council further stated, ". . . many black Americans remain separated from the mainstream of national life under conditions of great inequality" (p. 4).

Statistics on median income, rates of poverty, and employment support these findings (*The Economic Report of the President*, 1997). The median income for white families was $42,646 in 1995. However, the median income for African-American families that same year was only $25,970. The percentage of white families living below the poverty level in 1995 was 8.5%. African-American families living in poverty totaled 26.4% in 1995, a rate more than three times that of whites. Finally, civilian unemployment for African Americans (9.6%) was nearly two times that of whites (4.9%) in 1995.

The current economic status of many African Americans appears to replicate conditions which existed almost 30 years ago. In 1968, the Kerner Commission released a report with findings similar to those above (*Report of the National Advisory Commission on Civil Disorders*, 1968). The commission had been formed by President Lyndon Johnson to study the causes of the 1967 riots, which had taken place in 150 cities. It stated that

the unemployment rate among African Americans was double that of whites
while the median income of African Americans was slightly more than half
that of whites. The report indicated that this economic disparity was an
important factor contributing to the urban riots. It further predicted that
unless steps were taken to ameliorate this disparity, "within two decades this
division could be so deep that it would be almost impossible to unite" (p.
407).

On April 29, 1992, South Central Los Angeles erupted in riots not
unlike the 1965 riots in Watts, a South Central neighborhood. The overt
reason was the sense of injustice resulting from the acquittal of police
officers who had beaten a resident, Rodney King. However, subsequent
analyses focused on underlying economic and social conditions (Hazen,
1992).

South Central Los Angeles had suffered substantial job losses due to
plant closings. Between 1979 and 1982, 15 major plants closed, resulting
in the loss of nearly 22,000 jobs in this community (Hazen, 1992). One of
the federal programs which retrains workers who lose jobs as a result of
plant closings is the Job Training Partnership Act. However, in 1988, the
level of expenditure per person in South Central was only $49. This figure
was 55% less than was spent per person in West Los Angeles, 28% less
than in Central Los Angeles, and 22% less than in the Valley.

Disparities existed in other areas as well. The earnings gap between
comparable African-American men and white men in Los Angeles during
the period 1986 to 1987 was 30% . The poverty rate for South Central was
30.3% in 1992, more than three times the national average. Finally, the ratio
of residents to stores in Los Angeles County in 1990 was 203 to 1. In South
Central, this ratio was 415 to 1.

The riots of 1965, 1967 and 1992 came to be viewed by many policy
analysts as a response to the disparity in the economic status of African
Americans and whites. The recommendation by the Kerner Commission in
1968 and by policy makers following both periods of unrest was to promote
business ownership among African Americans. However, little was said
about the rationale for using enterprise as a vehicle for economic
development. In short, how does business ownership affect economic
development and how is economic development defined? The next section
explains this relationship.

Economic Development and Business Ownership

Economic development is often thought of as creating jobs, increasing flows of income to individuals and communities, and increasing the tax base to allow improvements in such areas as the housing stock, the educational system, and the infrastructure. In fact, these are the outcomes of economic development (Green & Pryde, 1989; Vaughan & Bearse, 1981).

Economic development is the creation of change in the market place. Entrepreneurs can be initiators of such change. Entrepreneurs can create competition in the market place and challenge existing firms. They may improve productivity, efficiency, quality, and consumer choice while lowering prices (Daniels, Barbe, & Lirtzman, 1981; Vesper, 1983). They seek out unsatisfied needs in the market and meet them. They accelerate the advancement and dissemination of technology. Additionally, they may attract investment which leads to job creation for people who may not fit in existing organizations. And they contribute to tax revenues and decentralize economic power.

This study will primarily address small business ownership. For the purposes of this research, small business is defined as sole proprietorships, partnerships, and Subchapter S corporations (a classification of corporations established by the Internal Revenue Service).

The following sections will provide a history of business ownership by African Americans.

Historical Perspective

This section lays the groundwork and places in context the policy proposals for African-American economic development which have been espoused from the 1960s to date. It will become clearer during the course of this paper that the options for economic development offered from the 1960s forward have not been new ones; rather, they have reasserted alternatives espoused by African Americans for centuries. Similarly, the issues which have raised heated debate during the 1960s and at present are not new either. These same issues were the source of equally intense disputes in prior decades.

In studying African-American economic development, many researchers have contended that African Americans do not have a history of entrepreneurship or saving for business investment (Frazier, 1971; Green & Pryde, 1989; Light, 1972; Tabb, 1970). John Sibley Butler (1991) has presented a convincing argument opposing this view. He has provided a detailed account of how African Americans have used entrepreneurship to promote their self-sufficiency from the time they set foot in America.

Even researchers, such as Butler, who have documented the history of African Americans in business, rarely examine African influence on their economic development. One researcher who did investigate this influence was W.E.B. Du Bois (1907); he stated the following:

> It used to be assumed in studying the Negro American that in any development we might safely begin with zero so far as Africa is concerned; the later studies are more and more convincing us that this former attitude has been wrong, and that always in explaining the development in America of the Negro we must look back upon a considerable past development in Africa. We have, therefore, first to ask ourselves in this study, how far are the traces in Africa of economic life and economic-cooperation among Negroes. (p. 12)

The history of economic development in Africa is extensive and wide ranging. Around 500 B.C., Africa began its Iron Age (Davidson, 1968). Iron extractive and forging industries grew up south of the Sahara around 300 B.C. and, by 200 B.C., a major handicraft industry in iron developed on the Middle Nile, from which products were distributed widely. Over time, the economic organization within Africa developed such that villages were located in groups (Du Bois, 1907). Each village specialized in a product or service. For example, in what is now the Democratic Republic of the Congo, one village produced iron and copper goods while another village fished. Another village produced wine and yet another conducted the trade between the rest of the villages and supplied products made outside of the community of villages. The activities of the villages were reciprocal and complementary. It was understood that no village would produce goods or services outside of its sphere of specialization without being ostracized.

Not only did villages in close proximity establish trading links, but trading centers located in different regions of the continent developed long distance trading systems (Davidson, 1968). In the 14th century, cities such as Niani, the capital of the Mali empire in the upper Niger, organized the import of gold and other goods from regions to the south. Markets were established in the forestland to export produce from that area and purchase goods from other regions. Benin, in western Africa, grew into a powerful trading center in the 15th century as a result of the exchange of locally manufactured cotton goods for copper from the Sahara and horses from the Sudan. By 1400, ". . . the whole of West Africa [was] intricately traced with trading trails and market centers" (p. 66).

In addition to the well-established economic system for internal African trade, Africa also has a long history of international trade and economic development. East African iron gained an international reputation for its superior quality and good price as of the 12th century. It was traded to Sicily and throughout India. Also during the 12th century, within the city of Timbuktu in West Africa, a city known as a center of learning, there existed a large market for manuscript books. More profit was made from the sale of books than from any other merchandise. Taghaza, also a West African trading city, was a salt manufacturing center, and the Sudanese city of Sijilmasa was the crossroad for western trade in gold on which Europe based its monetary system. East African international trade consisted of the export of metals and ivory in exchange for cotton with countries such as China.

This discussion has offered examples of economic systems that existed in both East and West Africa. Most African Americans are believed to be descendants of Africans brought to America from the western part of Africa. Therefore, it could be argued that any economic influences came primarily from West Africa. However, as indicated above, the considerable travel and trade across regions of the continent provided an opportunity for the exchange of customs between those living in the East and West. Further research would be required to verify this.

A more extensive discussion of the history of African economic organization and enterprise is beyond the scope of this book. However, it is important to establish that African-American economic organization did not begin with their entry into America. In order to fully understand African-American economic development, one must recognize the African influence.

The enslavement and movement of African people to America and the subsequent process of dehumanization destroyed a great deal of African culture. Yet some institutions and traditions remained intact and were perpetuated both during the period of enslavement and thereafter (Du Bois, 1907; Puryear & West, 1973). The following is a discussion of some of the economic institutions, spokesmen, and issues important to the foundation of African-American economic development.

The Church

One of the oldest institutions influenced by African tradition was the African-American church. As one of the few surviving African social institutions, the church assumed many of the functions of other institutions that had been suppressed by American society (Du Bois, 1907). It became the focal point of economic activity as well as education and religion.

These churches were formed as early as the 1700s when free African Americans withdrew from white churches in the face of discrimination. Enslaved African Americans also formed their own churches. A third impetus arose from white churches opting to form separate churches for their African-American members. These African-American churches were self-sustaining, self-governing, and for the most part economically autonomous. As they grew in numbers and membership between the late 1700s and the early 1900s, their property value and annual income grew into the millions. For example, between 1787 and 1903, the number of African Methodist Episcopal Churches grew from 1 to 5,831 (Butler, 1991; Du Bois, 1907). Their membership climbed from 42 to 759,590, and their property value increased from $2,500 to $9,405,000. (Note that since the dollar amounts have not been adjusted for inflation, the value would be much greater in current dollars.)

Once this economic base was established, these churches then began to develop schools. In the face of the many obstacles to African-American education, including laws forbidding the education of slaves, laws prohibiting the attendance of African Americans in public schools with whites, and the prohibitive cost and discrimination of private white schools, the churches provided and financed locations, materials, and instructors for educational institutions. These institutions included adult night schools as well as day schools, colleges, and universities.

Between 1847 and 1904, the African Methodist Episcopal Church gave more than $1 million to institutions of higher education (Butler, 1991). By

1907, it supported 22 schools, including high schools and colleges in the United States, Africa, and the Caribbean. Other churches also provided assistance. The Afro-American Baptist Church helped to support 107 schools of different educational levels in 1909.

In addition to fostering schools, the church made possible the establishment and maintenance of other institutions based on African tradition—secret societies and mutual benefit societies.

Secret Societies

Secret societies such as the Masons, Odd Fellows and Knights of Pythias grew out of the church (Du Bois, 1907). Again being prevented from joining those lodges organized by whites, African Americans founded their own. Prince Hall obtained a charter for the Free Masons from England in 1796. These lodges, through their dues, commanded substantial sums of money, as well as property, for that period and established practices such as payment of insurance to widows and orphans of deceased members. They also established widows' and orphans' homes and homes for the elderly and purchased land for cemeteries.

The income collected and benefits paid out were substantial for that period (Butler, 1991). In 1886, the Odd Fellows paid $37,757 to sick members, $21,002 for funeral expenses, and $6,957 to widows. They also donated $4,327 to charities, invested $100,993 in property, and had a balance of funds totaling $343,198. The Masons had a total income of $500,000 and property valued at well over $1 million in 1909.

Mutual Benefit Societies

A third institution influenced by African tradition was the African-American mutual benefit society. Initially, the societies were secretly formed and maintained by the slaves. In the early 1800s, "there existed in every city of any size in Virginia organizations of Negroes having as their objective the caring for the sick and the burying of the dead" (Du Bois, 1907). Despite laws prohibiting the assembly of African Americans unless a white person was present, slaves engineered ways of organizing, making payments, and maintaining records of participants using a numerical code system to protect the identity of the participants. When a member of the society became ill or died, the funds were used to care for or bury the member.

After emancipation, open mutual benefit societies were formed. Their members paid a weekly or monthly amount and, in turn, members who became sick received a weekly benefit (one society paid for half of the doctor's expense). In the case of death, the member's burial expense would be paid and the widow and children received benefits (Du Bois, 1907). One such society, the New York City Benevolent Society, was established in 1808. By 1900 it had real estate valued at over $40,000 and had receipts of over $3,000 (Butler, 1991).

Insurance Companies

Mutual benefit societies "laid the groundwork for one of the first successful business enterprises among Afro-American entrepreneurs—the insurance business" (Butler, 1991, p. 109). African Americans initially took out insurance in white companies. However, when they discovered that benefits paid them were smaller than those paid to whites for the same premium, they began establishing their own companies from the mutual benefit societies that already existed (Du Bois, 1907). These insurance companies did so well in Virginia that the state legislature passed measures intended to limit if not eliminate them. Yet, in the early 1900s, African-American companies outnumbered white companies despite the laws.

In 1931, African-American insurance companies had an income of $13,967,000 (Butler, 1991). These businesses were very well managed and strong enough to ride out the Great Depression. By 1937, more than 9,000 persons were employed by these companies, earning more than $4,810,000 in salaries and benefits. The National Negro Insurance Association had 62 member companies by 1948, which held nearly $1 billion worth of insurance in force, $108 million in assets, and had $55 million in annual income.

Several of these companies still exist today. Fourteen of the top 15 African-American insurance companies in 1994 were established prior to 1950; the oldest was established in 1899 ("B.E. Insurance Companies," 1995). They had $19 billion worth of insurance in force and $694 million in assets.

Banks

Banks were an outgrowth of the insurance companies (Du Bois, 1907). As the funds held by the benefit and insurance companies grew in size, they needed a repository for their funds. Consequently, African-American banks were formed to house this and other money from the community.

The first private African-American bank of substance was established in 1888 in the heart of Washington, DC's business district (Butler, 1991). In 1926, 33 African-American banks held over $12 million in total resources. These numbers dwindled markedly after the Depression to one bank with $406,012 in resources in 1932.

Cooperative Businesses

Cooperative businesses began during slavery, too. In instances when slave owners provided their slaves with small plots of ground for their own farming, the slaves would grow and sell produce (Du Bois, 1907). The gains from these sales would be used to purchase their freedom when possible. As they became free, either through this kind of payment or through escape, they would band together and pool their monies in order to purchase the freedom of others. This pooling of monies led to the development of businesses of all types, including building and loan associations and realty companies often organized by beneficial and insurance societies; newspapers, such as Fredrick Douglass' *North Star*, department stores; drug stores; manufacturers; and contractors.

The African tradition of cooperative economics was sustained by African Americans during and after slavery. When slavery ended, many freedmen sought to gain their economic emancipation by pooling their assets, buying farms, purchasing land at tax sales, and taking advantage of homestead acts which made land available in Alabama, Mississippi, and Louisiana. One advocate of economic development through land ownership and business ownership was Booker T. Washington.

Booker T. Washington

Booker T. Washington, himself a former slave, believed that the most effective means by which African Americans could make the transition from slavery to full emancipation was through economic achievement. He stated that "economic efficiency [is] the foundation of every kind of success" (1909, p. 192). Toward that end, he founded Tuskegee Normal and Industrial Institute in 1881. At a time when most African-American colleges were run by whites, Tuskegee had an all African-American faculty as well as student body (Harlan, 1968). The school taught agricultural science and industrial skills with the intention of preparing students to become profitable landowners and entrepreneurs (Armstrong, 1974; Washington, 1909). Washington promoted the training of hands as well as heads and believed that industrial education was closely correlated with economic achievement among the masses of African Americans (Mathews, 1971).

Washington offered a program that he believed would counter the despair of African Americans as the gains of Reconstruction were reversed by peonage, lynchings, the Black Codes, and Jim Crow laws (Hawkins, 1974; Washington, 1909). In the face of such political losses, he asserted that "the only sure basis of progress is economic" (Washington, 1907, pp.269-270). He believed that African Americans would find greater possibilities in business than in politics and that the business world held opportunities that were closed to them in other arenas (Harlan, 1968; Washington, 1909).

Washington urged former slaves to capitalize on skills they had used during slavery, such as carpentry and cooking, by establishing businesses in contracting, catering and restauranteuring (Washington, 1907). During slavery, African Americans had few opportunities to engage in business on their own behalf and, due to laws prohibiting teaching slaves to read, write, or calculate, it was often impossible for them to engage in business for the slave owners. However, following the end of slavery, Washington viewed the South as a good place for African Americans to enter business. Unlike the North, the South did not have a large number of highly organized, competitive businesses at that time. African Americans, in his opinion, could enter the business world and grow gradually without being forced out by competition early on.

In 1900, Washington formed the Negro Business League for the purposes of (a) sharing information among African-American businessmen and (b) encouraging more African Americans to enter into business across the country. The League developed many affiliates in different parts of the country.

In attempting to bring about economic self-sufficiency for African Americans, Washington used a strategy of cooperation with white Southerners (Mathews, 1971). He appealed to whites for funding to build separate African-American institutions such as Tuskegee. He felt that as African Americans achieved success in business based on their training in such institutions and as whites became more enlightened, the separation of the races would dissipate and integration would be achieved (Harlan, 1968; Washington, 1907). Washington did develop many white benefactors for his various institutions, among them Carnegie and Rockefeller. Even so, the white community as a whole responded not with cooperation, but with de jure segregation in the South and de facto segregation in the North (Mathews, 1971). As a consequence, an increasing number of African Americans began to criticize Washington's conciliatory approach. Among his best known and most ardent critics was W.E.B. Du Bois.

W. E. B. Du Bois

William Edward Burghart Du Bois was born a freeman in Massachusetts in 1868. Unlike Washington, who for the most part pursued a consistent economic philosophy, Du Bois' views on full African-American emancipation evolved over time (Meier, 1971). His interest in African-American business enterprise was clearly demonstrated by his early work, including a survey he conducted on African-American-owned businesses while on the faculty at Atlanta University in 1898.

The intent of the study was to determine the number, type and longevity of these businesses as well as the amount of their capital investment (Du Bois, 1971). He operationally defined businessmen as those who had made a capital investment of at least $500 in their business. Du Bois estimated there were 5,000 such businesses in the country at that time, and his survey covered 1,906 of these. His study indicated that approximately $9 million of capital had been invested by African-American businessmen. While small in comparison to amounts invested in American business overall, Du Bois viewed this amount as a substantial investment in light of the short period of time that had elapsed since the abolition of slavery. With regard to longevity of businesses, he found that caterers, florists, builders, contractors, barbers and market gardeners had been established the longest.

Du Bois concluded that the greatest obstacle to African-American entry into the competitive business world was the shifting of that business world from one of small capitalists to large industries, department stores and trusts. While small white capitalists faced the same problem, African-American businessmen also faced an entry barrier to inclusion and employment in these larger businesses:

> A Negro can to-day [*sic*] run a small corner grocery with considerable success. To-morrow [*sic*], however, he cannot be head of the grocery department of the department store which forces him out of business. (p. 25)

Du Bois set forth the original concept for a Negro Businessmen's League (Harlan, 1968), with the intent to promote African-American entrepreneurship and the patronage of these businesses by African Americans. Later that same year, Du Bois was made director of a bureau on African-American business and given responsibility for organizing business leagues. However, it was Washington who actually brought the National Negro Business League into being in 1900.

Not only did Du Bois conduct the above-mentioned survey on businesses, he also carried out a study in 1907 on cooperative economics among African Americans. In that study, Du Bois showed how African Americans had instituted an economic organization during slavery based on African tradition which developed into businesses after emancipation.

In spite of Du Bois' demonstrated interest in African-American economic development, by 1903 his writing clearly established his belief that the struggle for the right to vote (political power), civil rights, and higher education was primary while economic achievement was secondary (Du Bois, 1903). Du Bois and Washington were to debate this point for years to come.

Du Bois became a leading advocate of political and civil rights through his organization of the Niagara Movement and its successor, the National

Association for The Advancement of Colored People (Broderick, 1974; Du Bois, 1940, 1969; Mathews, 1971; Meier, 1971). In his view, for African Americans to seek economic achievement as a primary goal rather than political, civil, and educational rights was to sacrifice self-respect for land and houses (Du Bois, 1903). Economic gains could not be protected without the vote and equal access.

In contrast, Washington believed that African-American progress could best be obtained through cooperation rather than confrontation with whites. Economic enterprise met this criterion. Through entrepreneurship, African Americans could achieve even in the face of segregation.

In his later years, Du Bois again turned to economic development as an approach to improving the quality of life for African Americans. He believed that the key to the social hierarchy in America was wealth. He defined this as ". . . income and oligarchic economic power, the consequent political power and the prestige of those who own and control capital and distribute credit" (Du Bois, 1940, p. 189).

Du Bois' central thesis was that it was necessary for African Americans to provide the funding themselves for addressing problems they faced. Du Bois proposed an economic alternative based on traditional African communalism. He argued that there existed African Americans trained and skilled to meet every need. These trained persons could be brought together to form cooperative wholesale and manufacturing establishments that would provide the goods and services needed by African Americans.

In addition, Du Bois asserted the need to develop consumer power. He viewed the consumer as replacing the producer as the most powerful voice in industry. African Americans should organize and help shape the economy through their purchasing power, thereby gaining some democratic control over industry. Central to the shaping of a new economy would be the building of "new economic institutions suited to minority groups . . ." (p. 209).

In his early writings on cooperative economics among African Americans, Du Bois documented a history in which African Americans, when discriminated against in activities by the larger society, pooled their resources and formed their own institutions and services, including churches, schools, and insurance companies (Du Bois, 1907). By 1940 he was proposing that African Americans use their power as consumers and their wide-ranging skills to form cooperatives, provide goods and services for themselves where possible, build economic autonomy, and deal with the larger society from a position of strength in obtaining those goods and services which they could not feasibly provide for themselves.

Reasons for Limited Presence of African-American Firms

African-American institutions provided a unique economic system both during and after the period of slavery. Following slavery, individuals and organizations set about to promote African-American economic self-sufficiency through entrepreneurship as well as cooperative business efforts. Yet, by the 1960s, as noted earlier in this chapter, the economic status of members of this group was well below that of their white counterparts. African Americans were also grossly underrepresented among business owners. In 1969, 163,073 African-American businesses had 151,996 paid employees (Bates, 1973a). Their sales totaled $4.5 billion, or about $27,500 per firm on average. This represented approximately 1.36% of all businesses in the United States (U.S. Bureau of the Census, 1975).[1]

Several factors contributed to the limited number of businessmen, including racial discrimination, limited access to potential customers, downturns in the national economy, and insufficient education.

During the antebellum period, African Americans in the North were engaged in most areas of business, and some were very successful (Lee, 1973). However, southern white society accepted African-American businesses only in the area of personal service, such as catering and barbering (Bates, 1973a; Du Bois, 1971). Other areas, such as merchandising, were viewed as inappropriate and off limits for African Americans. The formation of such enterprises was inhibited by laws which forbade African Americans to engage in businesses which required a knowledge of reading and writing and by acts of violence against businesses and their owners. These acts of violence were not limited to the South; they were also quite common in northern cities such as Boston, Philadelphia, and Chicago.

The relatively small number of African-American businessmen resulted also from limited access to customers. Prior to the Civil War, most patrons of African-American enterprises were white. However, the animosity which flourished after the war and the subsequent development of a segregated society ended white patronage of these businesses. At that time, most African Americans lived in the South, so there was not a sufficiently large community in the North to patronize these businesses. Even in the South, access to the African-American market was limited since a great many people were sharecroppers and had to buy from the landlord's store.

Economic conditions further limited the number of African-American businesses. Due to their recent status as slaves and the post-war depression in the South, few African Americans had the capital to establish businesses that required substantial investment. Banks were unwilling to provide them with the loans they needed. Without capital or credit, African Americans were unable to make the conversion from personal service to industrial age businesses (Lee, 1973). On top of these constraints, in the aftermath of the Panic of 1873, very few African-American businesses survived.

World War I brought African Americans to the North to fill jobs. The income from these jobs provided the capital they needed to form businesses, and the mass exodus to the North established the communities needed to support them (Bates, 1973a; Drake & Cayton, 1971). By 1929, African-American businesses were commonplace not only in personal service but in new lines such as the printing industry. In 1932, retail businesses alone numbered 25,701 in areas as diverse as car dealerships, apparel, furniture, building supplies and hardware, as well as the more common food stores and restaurants (Butler, 1991). These businesses had an annual trade of more than $101 million in 1932.

However, the Great Depression followed closely on the heels of this business boom. While many white businessmen were able to obtain the credit they needed to sustain them through the depression, African Americans were not, and much of the growth which had occurred was wiped out.

It is not clear why there has not been more growth in the number of African-American businesses since the Depression. Little information exists on the period from the late 1930s through the mid 1960s about these firms (Bates, 1973a). Joseph Pierce's survey of 12 cities in 1944 does provide systematic documentation of businesses in some parts of the country (Butler, 1991). Among these cities, he found 1,556 African-American retail stores which averaged 2.8 paid employee each, 1,766 service establishments which averaged 2.3 paid employees, and 352 miscellaneous businesses with 9.1 paid employees on average (insurance companies led the latter group with a mean of 24.4 employees). By and large, the research done during this period concluded that African-American firms were typically small, and their owners cited difficulty in obtaining credit as a major impediment to their ability to compete (Bates, 1973a).

A possible explanation for the lack of growth was offered by Butler (1991). He asserted that legal segregation impeded the African-American businesses' expansion in a way that no other entrepreneurial group was affected. African Americans have been the only group in this country prevented, by law, from competing in the open market.

Butler's view runs counter to the often-argued position that the end of legal segregation created greater competition for African-American firms; consequently, these firms were unable to survive. Brimmer and Terrell (1971) asserted that African-American businesses were able to exist in the past because racial segregation provided a protected market for the provision of services within the African-American community.

This latter position is flawed in two ways. First, it presents a one-sided analysis which fails to examine the negative impact of segregation on African-American businesses (Bates, 1973a; Butler, 1991; Tate, 1971). As previously stated, prior to the Civil War, these firms served a predominantly white clientele. Segregation put an end to their access to this market. They were limited to developing business solely within the confines of the African-American community.

The second flaw in this argument is that white businesses were never completely excluded from conducting business with African Americans (Bates, 1973a). Historically, when white businessmen found it profitable to target the African-American market, they did so, increasing the competition for African-American firms. In view of the limitations to the Brimmer and Terrell (1971) argument, it appears that Butler's explanation of limited access to the open market may be a major reason for the relatively small number of African-American businesses.

A final explanation offered by researchers for the limited presence of these firms since the Depression is level of education. On the one hand, a lack of education may have prevented African-Americans from making further inroads in business (Drake & Cayton, 1971; Farley, 1981). A college education in any field was out of reach for most African Americans prior to the 1960s, and access to college business schools was even more limited. The percentage of African Americans age 25 and older with four or more years of college was 1.3 in 1940, 2.2 in 1950, and 3.5 in 1960 (National Center for Education Statistics, 1994). By comparison, these rates for whites were 4.9, 6.6 and 8.1, respectively.

On the other hand, of those who were able to obtain a college education, relatively few chose to go into business (Bates, 1973a). Their choices may have been due in part to limited access to investment capital even with a college degree. Another explanation is that the initial financial return may have been greater for new graduates who went to work for someone else than for graduates who invested in their own businesses. Butler (1991) pointed out that entrepreneurial activities of immigrants decline with each successive generation. Similarly, African-American entrepreneurs from the early 1900s may have wanted professional and other careers for their children.

These reasons for limited African-American business growth since World War II are largely speculative. Additional research is required to clearly establish the basis for this limited growth. Another area needing further research is the current practices of African Americans regarding the pooling of resources for economic self-sufficiency and business enterprises. Du Bois clearly established a history of this custom, but no research resembling his work has been conducted in recent years. It is not feasible to pursue such an investigation in this study. These are areas for future research.

II

Economic Development Models and Legislation

The previous chapter examined the history of African-American economic development. It concluded that while African Americans had a long-term presence in business, they were still underrepresented in the 1960s. This chapter examines some of the policy debates from the 1960s forward and also presents a summary of current public policies and programs affecting small and minority-owned businesses. Recent legislative and judicial actions relevant to these polices and programs are then discussed.

Alternative Proposals for Economic Development

The riots of 1967 drove home the fact that what happened in the African-American community had a tremendous impact on the rest of the nation. In response, a flood of proposals and programs were advanced to increase the growth of African-American business ownership. Following the Los Angeles riots in 1992, several legislative measures were again introduced in Congress.

Underlying these proposals was the belief that business ownership would lead to economic advancement in African-American communities (Brimmer & Terrell, 1971; Cross, 1969; Farley, 1981; Kelso & Hetter, 1971; Tabb, 1970). The basis for this belief sprang from a wide variety of perceptions about the consequences of business ownership, including that business ownership would result in job creation, increased social stability, and economic integration into the mainstream (Bates, 1974). In essence, it was thought that entrepreneurship and business ownership by African Americans would spark economic development in this community in the same way such events would occur in the mainstream society.

The following sections describe four major economic development models advanced during the last 25 years.

The Black Capitalism Model

Advocates of private-enterprise capitalism perceived African-American economic development in the inner city as lacking three essential components: credit at reasonable rates, risk capital, and business skill (Cross, 1969; McKersie, 1971; McNeish, 1969). As a means of correcting this absence of essential economic elements, several private-ownership supporters proposed a series of federally funded financial incentives that would accrue primarily to white corporations willing to assist the inner city in obtaining credit, capital and business skill (Sturdivant, 1971).

The underlying rationale was that corporate America held the resources required to build a stronger business sector in the inner city. However, corporations considered such an investment of resources risky and cost inefficient. Consequently, these corporations would have to be provided an incentive to invest.

The proposed incentives would take the form of federal tax credits and deductions and increased Federal Deposit Insurance Corporation (FDIC) coverage. Special additions to bad debt reserves were proposed for institutions willing to provide credit and risk capital to the inner city. Tax incentives were also proposed for businesses offering to enhance the skills of existing and potential businessmen in the inner city through corporate-sponsored training programs and entrepreneurial development centers. Another recommendation for improving the business skills of African Americans was for corporations to provide them with franchises. These corporations would, in turn, receive a tax credit for franchise income from the inner-city franchiser. Finally, it was proposed that the federal government preside over the transfer of some large, white-owned corporations to African-American ownership (America, 1971). The original owner would be compensated for the full market value of the property with public funds.

Many African Americans who addressed economic development had a considerably different view of the world than white corporate America. From the viewpoint of the former, the poor economic status of African Americans stemmed from their limited control of the institutions that had an impact on their lives (Innis, 1969). Such institutions included entities that controlled the flow of goods and services within their communities. These spokespersons believed that the past failures of economic development programs aimed at African Americans were due to their exclusion as decision makers. Previous programs were seen as having been developed by whites to meet their own needs.

What was needed were alternatives not only developed by African Americans but also controlled by them. This was a period in which African Americans were demanding self-determination and community control. Those who held this perspective proposed the alternative of cooperative ownership of economic resources by members of the African-American community.

The Cooperative Ownership Model

The cooperative ownership proposal which had the potential for the broadest impact was the Community Self-Determination Act of 1968 (*Harvard Law Review*, 1971; Innis, 1969; McClaughry, 1969; Sturdivant, 1971). A coalition of people designed this bill, including leaders of the Congress on Racial Equality (CORE), aides to President Nixon, Republican and Democratic members of Congress, and economists. The intent of the bill was to establish community owned and directed corporations that would control the economic and social development of designated urban and rural areas. The community development corporations (CDCs) were meant to increase the community's ownership of productive capital and property. They would acquire, create, and manage businesses in the designated areas. The residents of the areas were to be the stockholders in the CDCs.

A series of tax incentives was included in the bill which would have encouraged entrepreneurs coming in from outside the designated areas to sell their businesses to the CDCs, once these businesses became viable. Banks, intended to provide the capital for the CDCs' purchase of businesses, would also have been created through the sale of debentures guaranteed by the federal government. The CDCs would also have had access to funds to hire managerial and technical expertise. Profits received by CDCs would have been used to help finance housing, day care, education, health, and recreation services for the community.

The Community Self-Determination Act was not passed by Congress. However, in 1971, Congress passed a similar measure, Title VII of the Community Economic Development Amendment to the Economic Opportunity Act of 1964. This legislation did establish CDCs as a partnership among the community, government, and private business sector that would develop special programs to combat poverty and develop economic stability.

A 1977 analysis of 13 CDCs drew less than glowing conclusions (Berndt, 1977). First, community control was found to be minimal. Outside specialists occupied most of the decision-making positions and the boards, while consisting primarily of residents, were largely middle class and thus were not representative of the poor residents. Second, the researchers pointed out that "if established business and industry cannot make it in the inner cities, how can inexperienced poor people make it? All of the minuses of these locations that caused business interests to move out still exist" (p. 130).

Third, physical development, which was intended to provide employment, improve the visual appearance of the community, and return investments through rents and sale of units, did not meet all objectives. Although new homes were built and existing ones renovated, the physical development corporations were not profitable.

Finally, corporations did not participate in the two capacities most needed. They failed to enter into joint ventures with the CDCs and to locate labor-intensive plants in the communities.

The Underdeveloped Nation Model

A third approach to African-American economic development and entrepreneurship was offered by individuals who thought the ghetto should be viewed as a totality—as an underdeveloped nation with a need for increased economic productivity and stability (Harrison, 1971; McLaurin, 1971; McLaurin & Tyson, 1969). These theorists criticized efforts focusing solely on employment training or the provision of capital and training for small businesses. Such approaches were regarded as piecemeal. The underdeveloped nation theorists' stated goal was "to redress the adverse balance of payments between the ghetto and the outer white world and to attain capital and profits under local control" (McLaurin & Tyson, 1969, p. 128).

Development economics characterized underdeveloped nations as having low per capita income; a small, weak middle class; low rates of increase in labor productivity, capital formation, and domestic savings; heavy dependence on external markets and few basic exports which faced an inelastic demand (i.e., an adverse balance of payments); limited local entrepreneurship; and heavy external ownership of local businesses (Tabb, 1970). Parallels were drawn between the characteristics of these nations and the inner cities, which faced low levels of income and savings, high unemployment, heavy nonresidential ownership of businesses, and limited African-American entrepreneurship. In addition, most goods and services were imported while the principal export, unskilled labor, faced an aggregate demand that did not increase at the rate of growth occurring in the labor force.

The objectives proposed by some of these theorists were to (a) transfer ownership from absentee owners to local minority owners; (b) develop an overall economic plan through which the community could participate in the planning and development of the community yet leave individual business development in the control of entrepreneurs; (c) enable the African-American community to compete in the economy of the larger society by diversifying, strengthening, and expanding its economic base; and finally d) increase the productivity of the African-American community by increasing its ownership of industries that produce, not merely distribute externally produced goods and services (McLaurin, 1971).

The Enterprise Zone Model

In the 1980s, the concept of enterprise zones was introduced. This strategy for stimulating economic development in disadvantaged urban areas used tax incentives and regulatory reduction to stimulate investment and local entrepreneurship (Butler, 1981).

In 1993, Congress passed the Empowerment Zone and Enterprise Community legislation following the unrest in South Central Los Angeles (Omnibus Budget Reconciliation Act, 1993). This law authorized the designation of six urban and three rural Empowerment Zones as well as 95 Enterprise Communities, 65 urban and 30 rural. Both Zones and Communities were eligible for tax-exempt facility bonds related to business enterprise activities. Each of the Communities received $3 million. Urban Zones received $100 million each in flexible Title XX Social Service Block Grants, which were discretionary funds from the Department of Health and Human Services. Rural areas received $40 million. Firms in Zones were also afforded some additional tax benefits. One important provision allowed them to increase their expensing deductions for plants and equipment to up to $20,000. In addition, they were able to receive employer wage credits of up to $3,000 per year per employee for wages and training expenses if the employee worked and lived in the community.

The U.S. Department of Housing and Urban Development (HUD) had responsibility for selecting urban sites and the U.S. Department of Agriculture (USDA) selected rural sites. Approximately 500 applications were submitted by communities from across the country. In addition to the Zones and Communities discussed above, these Departments also chose two supplemental Zones and four Enhanced Communities to receive HUD economic development grants. These designations were made in December 1994.

The proposed federal budget for fiscal year 1998 that White House budget submitted to Congress contained a provision to expand the number of designated areas (Budget of the United States Government, Fiscal Year 1998, 1997). Twenty additional Empowerment Zones and 80 Enterprise Communities would be selected, if passed by Congress.

Not all agree that enterprise zones provide the answer for distressed urban areas. Some have argued that the premise upon which this policy is based is not yet supported by empirical evidence. Additionally, business decisions to expand, relocate, or start up have been driven only secondarily by taxes (Berndt, 1977; Daniels, Barbe, & Lirtzman, 1981; Levitan & Miller, 1992). The primary determinants of such decisions have been the availability of a skilled labor force, the accessibility to markets, the appearance and safety of the physical environment, and the potential for maximizing profit.

Tax incentives have not directly improved the human capital and employability of the residents. Incentives have also been unlikely to influence small business start-ups since most owners have been unable to make use of incentives in their early years. Finally, there has been no guarantee that income produced by beneficiaries of the incentives would be reinvested in the communities and their residents.

Although federal legislation was passed only recently, 37 states had previously implemented enterprise zones (Levitan & Miller, 1992). The findings were not promising. Few small businesses were able to take advantage of tax incentives; consequently, they were at a disadvantage compared to larger businesses which could. Businesses had difficulty meeting requirements to hire residents since many residents had insufficient skills and there were no education and training provisions in the states' policies. The enterprise zones created few net businesses or jobs.

While proponents of the four models differ in their ideology and some of their strategies for economic development, there is a common denominator to each of the models. They all advocate increased business ownership by African Americans.

Current Policies and Programs

This section provides some background on public policies and programs that exist to assist small and minority-owned businesses. It is not intended to be exhaustive.

Small Business

The Small Business Act of 1953, as amended, states, "It is the declared policy of the Congress that the federal government, through the Small Business Administration [SBA], acting in cooperation with the Department of Commerce and other relevant state and federal agencies, should aid and assist small businesses. . . ." This law created the SBA as an administration under the general supervision of the president and not affiliated with any other agency or department of the federal government.

A central provision under this legislation is the 7(a) program, which makes financial assistance available to small businesses by guaranteeing loans made by banks and other lending institutions and, in some cases, through direct loans. These funds can be used to acquire land, plants, materials, and equipment or for working capital. SBA is considered a lender of last resort, and applicants must demonstrate an inability to obtain credit elsewhere. Minority-owned firms are also eligible for 7(a).

In 1958, the Small Business Investment Act established the Small Business Investment Company (SBIC) Program (Small Business Administration, 1977). The stated intent was to

> improve and stimulate the National economy in general and the small business segment thereof in particular, by establishing a program to stimulate and supplement the flow of private equity capital and long-term loan funds which small business concerns need for the sound financing of their business operations and for their growth, expansion and modernization, and which are not available in adequate supply . . . [with] maximum participation of private financing sources. (p. 1)

The SBICs are privately-owned and operated companies licensed by SBA. They can sell debentures guaranteed by SBA to raise funds for venture capital, long-term loans, and management consulting services for small businesses. SBICs are supposed to be profit-making corporations that pay dividends to their owners and raise additional private capital which can also be invested in small businesses (Small Business Administration, 1977). At the time the Program was created, it was intended to fill a gap in SBA's lending services by providing assistance whether or not small businesses were able to get short-term financing from commercial banks.

Minority-owned Business

In 1969 SBA made an administrative decision to reformulate section 8(a) of the Small Business Act to provide federal procurement contracts to minority-owned small businesses (Eddy, 1993). Prior to this time, this section authorized SBA to contract with *small* businesses; however, it had not been used. After section 8(a) was targeted to minority-owned firms, it grew rapidly. In 1978, Public Law 95-507 made this administrative change law.

The 8(a) Program is a business development program for socially and economically disadvantaged businesses. Socially disadvantaged individuals are defined as those who have experienced racial or ethnic prejudices or cultural bias (typically African Americans, Hispanic Americans, Native Americans, and Asian Americans). Economically disadvantaged people are those who are socially disadvantaged and whose ability to compete in the free market has been impaired due to diminished capital and credit opportunities. This program enables SBA to enter into contracts with other federal agencies for their procurement needs and then subcontract the work to eligible, SBA-certified firms. Firms can only remain in the program for nine years and are then expected to "graduate."

The 1978 legislation also required all federal agencies to set percentage goals for contracting with small, minority-owned firms. Each federal agency was also required to create an Office of Small and Disadvantaged Business Utilization (OSDBU) which would be responsible for each agency's contracting programs for small and disadvantaged businesses. Procurement goals were strengthened in 1988 when Public Law 100-656 required the president to establish government-wide procurement goals for minority-owned businesses. This goal was to be no less than 5% of all prime contracts.

In 1969 Executive Order 11458 created the Specialized Small Business Investment Companies or SSBICs (Eddy, 1993). This Order was given statutory authority in 1972 with the passage of the Small Business Investment Act Amendments. Like the SBICs, the SSBICs are privately owned companies located across the country. They too can sell debentures guaranteed by SBA to provide equity capital, long-term loans, and management assistance for expansion, modernization, and operating expenses. SSBICs also provide venture capital for start-up costs and research and development expenses. Unlike SBICs, these companies only assist small disadvantaged businesses.

The SBA is not the only federal agency which addresses the concerns of minority-owned businesses. The Minority Business Development Agency (MBDA) was established in 1969 as a result of Executive Order 11458 issued by President Richard Nixon (Eddy, 1993). This agency is located within the Department of Commerce and is the only federal agency with the sole responsibility of fostering the creation and growth of minority-owned businesses. The MBDA works with major corporations and governments on the federal, state, and local levels to increase their business with minority-owned firms. The Agency also funds Minority Business Development Centers (MBDC) and Indian Bureau Development Centers across the country. These centers provide management and technical assistance to minority entrepreneurs who need help establishing or expanding their firms. While the centers do not provide funding, they assist clients by identifying sources of financing and in preparing proposals for financing and bonding. Unlike SBA, MBDA services minority-owned businesses of any size, not just small firms.

In 1996, MBDA sustained substantial cuts in its budget and staffing. The budget fell from $40 million to $30 million, staffing declined from 90 to 33 people, and the number of development centers was reduced from over 100 to less than 50.

Several other agencies have responsibility for programs which provide financing and business to minority-owned firms. The Public Works Act of 1977 was the first law establishing specific percentage goals for procurement from minority-owned businesses (Eddy, 1993). It is administered by the Economic Development Agency within the Department of Commerce and requires at least 10% of all grant dollars for local public works projects to go to minority-owned businesses.

The Department of Defense is required by the National Defense Authorization Act of 1987 to award 5% of the total value of its procurement contracts to minority-owned firms, historically Black colleges and universities and other minority institutions (Eddy, 1993). Unlike SBA's 8(a) program, businesses do not have to be certified. When this Act was reauthorized in 1991, Congress also created the Mentor Protege Pilot Program through Section 831. Prime contractors are authorized to award noncompetitive subcontracts to socially disadvantaged businesses.

The Surface Transportation and Uniform Relocation Assistance Act of 1987 (reauthorized by the Intermodal Surface Transportation Efficiency Act of 1991) requires the Department of Transportation (DOT) to spend at least 10% of federal highway and transit funds with disadvantaged businesses (Eddy, 1993). This Agency is also required, by the 1987 and 1992 amendments to the Airport and Airway Improvement Act of 1982, to spend at least 10% of federal airport improvement funds with these firms. Finally, DOT's Short Term Lending Program provides working capital at prime interest rates, and the Bonding Assistance Program issues payment and performance bonds to disadvantaged businesses.

Other policies and agencies which foster minority business creation and development are as follows: the Department of Energy (Public Laws

101-101, 102-377, and 102-486); the Department of State (Public Law 101-246); the Department of the Treasury (Public Law 100-86); the Agency for International Development (Public Laws 100-461 and 101-167); the Environmental Protection Agency (Public Laws 99-499, 101-507, and 101-549); the Federal Deposit Insurance Corporation (Public Law 100-86); the National Aeronautics and Space Agency (Public Law 101-144); and the Resolution Trust Corporation (Public Laws 101-73 and 102-233) (Eddy, 1993).

Assessment of Current Policies and Programs

With so many laws on the books, one might wonder why there are not more African-American owned firms. First, it is important to note that the number of firms has increased substantially, from 163,073 in 1969 (Bates, 1973a) to 620,912 in 1992 (U.S. Bureau of the Census, 1996). When viewed as a percentage of total firms in the United States, African-American firms more than doubled, from 1.35[1] in 1969 to 3.60[2] in 1992. In fact, they increased in number at a faster rate (46%) between 1987 and 1992 than total businesses in the United States (26%). Receipts of African-American firms grew 63% during this period, from $19.8 billion to $32.2 billion. The rate of growth in receipts for all firms was comparable at 67% (from $1,995 billion to $3,324 billion). Thus, these policies do appear to have had a positive impact on the growth of African-American firms.

Second, the growth may have been greater if not for other career opportunities which opened up for African Americans. It was pointed out in the previous chapter that successive generations of African Americans may be selecting professional and managerial careers rather than pursuing business ownership. The civil rights era began in the 1950s and continued through the 1960s. During this time, jobs previously unavailable to African Americans opened up. African Americans, especially college graduates, may have chosen these new fields rather than entrepreneurship. Statistical data appear to support this line of thinking. In 1983, 5.6% of the people employed as managers or professionals in the United States were African American (U.S. Bureau of the Census, 1994). This percentage increased to 6.6 in 1993. When translated into actual numbers of people, over 800,000 more African Americans were employed in this field in 1993 than in 1983. Had even a fraction of this group become entrepreneurs, a striking increase in the number of African-American businesses would have occurred. Given these alternative occupations, the number of African-American firms may have declined if these policies and programs had not existed.

Another consideration is that many of the policies and programs discussed above, although intended to foster minority business growth and development, do not provide start-up capital. They provide loans, guarantees, and contracts to existing firms, but very few help new businesses get started. The policies and programs that do provide start-up capital have received relatively poor assessments.

The SBIC and SSBIC programs are examples. An evaluation of these programs from 1958 to 1975 resulted in the following findings (SBA, 1977).

- The number and profitability of SBICs declined. The number fell from 721 in 1964 to 369 in 1975. Of the 369, only 261 were actually operating. SSBICs increased from 22 in 1970 to 77 in 1975, but then leveled out. Profitability was a function of SBICs' size, with larger companies more profitable. Although the policy was intended to emphasize larger companies, SBA continued to license predominantly small SBICs.

- Participation of private equity sources in the SBIC industry diminished. SBA-funded debt increased from 9% of total assets in 1961 to 40% in 1973. Private capital decreased correspondingly; therefore, the goal of private institutional takeover of SBICs was not met.

- The flow of private equity capital and long-term loans to small business concerns was limited and insufficient. Only 0.2% of small businesses in existence at the time of the study were reached. Furthermore, the type of assistance was predominantly straight loans as opposed to capital stock investments. For SBICs, 76% of the total financing provided from 1958 to 1973 was in the form of loans. For SSBICs, the amount was 86%. The percentage of capital stock investment for SBICs fell from 30 in 1973 to 15 in 1975. For SSBICs, the drop was from 17% in 1971 to 11% in 1973.

- The administration and operation of the Programs were problematic. SBICs were committing a large number of regulatory violations.

In March of 1995, the Committee on Small Business of the House of Representatives held hearings on SBICs and SSBICs. The General Accounting Office provided its initial findings of its ongoing review of these programs (*Status of Small Business Investment Companies,* 1995). These findings indicated that in 1994, there were 186 SBICs and 94 SSBICs. Of these, 111 had violated regulations, for instance by making prohibited investments in real estate.

In 1994, SBA did license 37 new SBICs, which were heavily capitalized with private funds. However, no new SSBICS were licensed in that same year. Minority firms did not get the same infusion of potential venture capital for their investment companies that small businesses received.

In sum, since the enactment of public policies to support African-American business development, the number and percentage of these firms have grown. These policies appear to be having a positive influence on the growth of these firms, yet they remain underrepresented in the marketplace. This underrepresentation may be due to new opportunities for African Americans to enter other fields. It may also be due to the lack of effective policies addressing start-up capital.

An increase in the net number of African-American firms requires not only the survival of existing firms, but the entry of new firms into the marketplace. Current policies are directed primarily towards existing businesses. Without effective policies which provide start-up capital for new firms, the overall growth of African-American firms may be slow. This issue is explored more fully in succeeding chapters. The increase in African-American firms that has occurred under current policies may also be hampered by recent government actions. The next section will summarize some of these events.

Recent Legislative, Executive, and Judicial Action

Several recent actions by Congress, the White House and the Supreme Court have the potential to inhibit the establishment and growth of African-American businesses.

Loan guarantees, investment corporations, and procurement set-aside programs have not been the only vehicles used by the government to foster minority enterprises. Tax incentives have also been employed. One such incentive was created in 1978, when the Federal Communications Commission (FCC) introduced a policy to promote minority ownership of broadcasting facilities by making use of the existing Internal Revenue Code Section 1071 (*Background and Issues*, 1995). This section dated back to 1943 and allowed capital gains from the sale or exchange of property to be deferred in cases where the FCC certified the actions.

The 1978 policy offered FCC tax certificates to owners of broadcast facilities who voluntarily sold their facilities to minority individuals or minority-controlled entities. This policy was modified further in 1982 to cover investors who contributed to the stability of the capital base of a minority enterprise by (a) providing start-up capital to allow minorities to purchase broadcast or cable properties or (b) purchasing shares in minority-controlled entities within the first year after they were licensed to operate.

FCC issued 378 tax certificates under the Code Section 1071 between 1978 and 1995, of which 317 were for the sale of broadcast properties to minorities. Even though the majority of the certificates under this section were issued under the minority program, as of 1995 minorities only held 2.9% of all broadcast licenses. While this number is small, it represents a substantial increase over the 0.5% owned by minorities in 1978.

Supporters of the policy have argued that it allowed minorities to enter a business which was virtually closed to them until recent years (*Statement of Senator Carol Moseley-Braun*, 1995). There were no minority-owned radio stations until 1956 or minority-owned television stations until 1973. And FCC awarded its first new radio station license to a minority-owned company in 1974.

However, Congress repealed the Section 1071 minority ownership program in 1995 and made the repeal retroactive to January 1995. The elimination of this incentive is likely to hinder future acquisitions of broadcast properties by minorities and possibly reduce their presence in this industry.

The recent actions of the legislative, executive and judicial branches of government regarding affirmative action policies and programs also have the potential to negatively impact efforts to foster minority business development. Affirmative action is defined by the U.S. Commission on Civil Rights as any measure which was taken to correct past or present discrimination or to prevent future discrimination (Bruno, 1996). It addresses employment, education, housing, and public contracting.

In 1995, each of the three branches of government engaged in some activity with regard to affirmative action. Members of Congress introduced and held hearings on numerous bills designed to eliminate the use of race, color, national origin, or gender as a basis for granting preferential treatment in the provision of public employment, education, federal benefits, public contracting, or subcontracting by public contractors. These measures were not passed.

On March 7, 1995, President Clinton initiated a government-wide review of federal affirmative action programs to examine their design, effect, and fairness (Stephanopoulos & Edley, Jr., 1995). Among those reviewed were the federal procurement policies and practices. The review findings, reported July 19, 1995, included the following:

> We conclude that these programs have worked to advance equal opportunity by helping redress problems of discrimination and by fostering the inclusion needed to strengthen critical institutions, professions and the economy. In addition, we have examined concerns about fairness. The evidence shows that on the whole, the federal programs are fair and do not unduly burden nonbeneficiaries.(p.2)

While the report supported the continuation of affirmative action programs, it also proposed four new restrictions for procurement programs. The first was to tighten the economic disadvantage test. This would require that in determining a business owner's program eligibility, the value of the owner's home and spouse's assets be considered. The second proposal was to tighten the requirements for graduation from the 8(a) program. The nine-year limit for participation in the program would remain in place, but additional criteria would be developed to determine whether a firm should graduate earlier. For example, a cap on the total dollars of contracts might be a criterion. The third proposal would strengthen safeguards against business owners fraudulently claiming to be minority-owned. And the fourth restriction would attempt to reduce regional or industrial concentration. Such concentration has occurred when a federal agency awarded contracts to minority-owned businesses primarily within one area, such as construction. This provision would phase out sheltered competition

programs, such as 8(a), in those regions or industries which are receiving
several contract awards. These proposals may be intended to focus program
resources on legitimate minority-owned businesses which are not receiving
their share of contract awards. However, the recommendations might also
increase the difficulty that intended beneficiaries have in becoming and
remaining qualified for these program.

The president's review of affirmative action was overshadowed on
June 12, 1995, when the Supreme Court ruled on the *Adarand
Constructors, Inc. v. Peña* (1995) case. At issue was a subcontract for
highway construction in Colorado. The contract between the U.S.
Department of Transportation and the prime contractor, Mountain Gravel,
had a Subcontracting Compensation Clause. This clause provided a
financial incentive to the prime contractor to subcontract with small socially
and economically disadvantaged businesses. The prime contractor
subcontracted with a Hispanic firm, Gonzales Construction Company.
Adarand Constructors, Inc., complained to the courts that it was the low
bidder, but was denied the subcontract because of the clause (Verrilli, Jr.,
Lepow, Del Duca, & Jenner & Block, 1994). The Supreme Court failed to
uphold the policy and ruled that federal policies based on race must
withstand "strict scrutiny":

> . . . all racial classifications, imposed by whatever Federal, state or local
> government actor, must be analyzed by a reviewing court under strict
> scrutiny. In other words, such classifications are constitutional only if they
> are narrowly tailored measures that further compelling governmental
> interests. Because our decision today alters the playing field in some
> important respects, we think it best to remand the case to the lower courts
> for further consideration in light of the principles we have announced.
> (*Adarand Constructors, Inc. v. Peña,* 1995)

This ruling did not strike down any specific policy or program. It did,
however, lay the groundwork for numerous court challenges to policies and
programs intended to foster minority business enterprise.

Given the importance placed on business ownership and the
continuation of policy development around it, it is essential to know how
African-American-owned businesses have fared thus far and under what
circumstances they do well. Greater understanding of these factors will

inform public policy so that it can be used more effectively to advance African-American business ownership and economic development.

Notes

1. This estimate was calculated by dividing 163,073, the number of African-American firms cited by Bates for 1969, by 12,010,000, the total number of businesses in the United States in 1969, as estimated by the Bureau of the Census.

2. This estimate was calculated using Bureau of the Census estimates for the number of African-American firms (621,000) and the total number of firms in the United States (17,253,000).

III

Research on African-American Business Ownership

Several studies have examined the status of African-American businesses. A primary source of information on the number, size, and type of these businesses has been the Census Bureau's Survey of Minority-Owned Business Enterprises for 1969, 1972, 1977, and 1982. Researchers have analyzed these data in efforts to evaluate the progress of minority business ownership (Bates, 1984-85; Handy & Swinton, 1983, 1984; Markwalder, 1981; Stevens, 1984; Woolf, 1986). In examining these surveys, they found that overall growth in African-American businesses has been small. However, variation in growth has occurred across industries and between regions.

Previous Research

Research on overall growth showed that African-American business sales during the period between 1969 and 1972 increased by only 2.3%. This low growth contradicted predictions that the rate of growth would outpace the growth in gross national product (GNP) since the real GNP grew by 8.6% during this same period (Bates, 1973a). This slow rate of growth continued between 1972 and 1977 when it was 1.5%. The GNP growth for this period was 14.4%. Also, contrary to predictions, none of the African-American firms had grown enough by 1979 to enter the ranks of the *Fortune 500*. The smallest *Fortune 500* firm made $410 million in sales in 1979 while the largest African-American firm made $65 million in 1979. In 1977, only 716

African-American firms had sales of more than $1.0 million per year while 95,600 firms had sales of less than $5,000.[1]

During this period, employment created by African-American businesses also fell below expectations. One researcher concluded that these businesses were neither a large nor a rapidly growing source of employment for African Americans (Markwalder, 1981). The increase in employment by these businesses was 5.9% between 1952 and 1977, while total civilian employment grew by 10.8%. These businesses provided 0.18% of total employment in 1952 and 0.17% in 1977. If it is assumed that these firms employed only African Americans, then they still provided jobs for less than 2% of all employed African Americans in 1977.

A study of five cities—New York; Chicago; Washington, DC; Philadelphia; and Boston—showed that African-American businesses in the central city areas that had received SBA loans generated 24,919 jobs between fiscal years 1968 and 1973 (Bates, 1974).[2] However, 100,000 African-American members of the civilian labor force were unemployed in those cities during that same period. It was concluded that given the magnitude of unemployment in these cities, the number of jobs being created was small, but not inconsequential.

The importance of the jobs created by African-American firms was further emphasized by Bates (1993). He found that white owners of small businesses do not hire African Americans, even when these businesses are located in predominantly minority communities. On the other hand,

> . . . 96 percent of black-owned firms operating in urban minority neighborhoods employ a labor force that is largely minority. Even outside minority neighborhoods, in areas where most white-owned businesses have no minority workers at all . . . 97 percent of black employers in these same areas utilized minority workers (and in most cases minorities made up over 75 percent of the labor force). In short, their geographic separation from ghetto areas has not severed the employment link between black-owned businesses and black job seekers. (pp.3, 11, and 12)

Bates also pointed out that African-American firms in emerging lines of business are very different from the traditional firms. As a case in point, Reginald Lewis, the African-American founder of the TLC Group investment firm, bought the worldwide food company, Beatrice International, for $985 million in 1987 (Edmond, 1988). Beatrice is owned by the Lewis family, which controls more than 50 percent of its common stock. In 1994, the company had sales of $1.8 billion and employed 4,200 people ("B.E. Industrial/Service 100," 1995).

There were 15 African-American industrial and service firms that each had over $100 million in sales in 1994 ("B.E. Industrial/Service 100," 1995). These firms do business in high technology fields such as broadcasting, television production, computers, and systems integration. Other areas of business covered by these firms are publishing, advertising, food processing and distribution, soft-drink bottling, automobile dealerships, construction, and oil refining. These firms alone employ nearly 12,000 people.

There were also 15 African-American financial institutions with over $100 million in assets each during that same year ("B.E. Financial Companies," 1995). These banks employed nearly 2,000 people.

Another area of study has been the ability of African-American businesses to repay loans. A study of Chicago, Boston, and New York found that 44.0% of existing African-American businesses and 46.9% of new businesses that received SBA loans between fiscal years 1968 and 1973 were more than 60 days delinquent in their loan repayment (Bates, 1974). Furthermore, 26.2% of existing businesses and 35.2% of new businesses had already ceased operations or were closing down due to their inability to repay the SBA loans. A later study looked at SBA loan approvals for the Regular Business Loan Program and Equal Opportunity Loan Program (EOL) for the period of 1969 through 1978 (Bates, 1982). It found that 49.5% of SBA minority loan approvals were successful while 61.3% of nonminority loan approvals were successful in repaying loans.

The high rate of failure may be a reflection of the types of industries loan recipients entered. For example, personal service industries, in which African Americans are over-represented, are less likely to thrive than other types of businesses (Bates, 1973b).

It has been argued that these high delinquency rates were directly attributable to the philosophy of the EOL program requiring minority loan recipients to be bad credit risks (Bates, 1982). It has further been argued that in an attempt to rapidly increase the number of minority businesses, initially SBA ". . . indiscriminantly provided financial assistance to poorly qualified applicants . . ." (Scott & Jensin, 1977, p. 44).

In addition to findings on rate of loan payment delinquencies, some studies also provided information on the formation (i.e., start-up) and failure (closing down) rates of minority businesses. A study by Stevens (1984) compared the business formation and failure rates of African Americans with Hispanics and Asian Americans. He determined that the failure rates were approximately the same across these groups. What differed was the formation rate, which was lower for African Americans than the other groups. This rate for African Americans was 15% compared to 17% for Hispanic Americans and 21% for Asian Americans.

Ando (1986) found that classic conditions to entry as well as minority-specific factors all played a role in determining the formation rates of minority businesses. The classic conditions associated with increased minority business formation were (a) rapid growth in demand in the industry; (b) low capital intensity; (c) low concentration (i.e., total receipts for the industry were not received by only a small number of firms in the industry); and (d) high growth in demand in the local geographic area. The minority-specific factors were the supply of entrepreneurs, SBA loans for minorities, and the business knowledge and experience of the owners. Another possible factor, which this study did not examine, is the packaging of assistance. For example, the combination of financial assistance with training may have increased formation of businesses.

To this point, the studies discussed have taken a broader look at rates of growth, failure, and formation of African-American businesses overall. Research has also looked more closely at the variation in the growth of African-American businesses to determine what factors are associated with increase.

Ong (1982) examined factors influencing variation in the prevalence of African-American business ownership in 1972, across 30 Standard Metropolitan Statistical Areas (SMSA). He assessed whether these business sectors were constrained on the supply or demand side. The results of the study indicated that constraints were on the supply side. That is, the supply of African-American businesses was limited by the lack of capital.

A significant factor was lack of access to loans. A second factor was called the "portfolio effect," meaning banks tended to perceive loans to African Americans as risky and preferred to hold portfolios with few loans to these business owners. There was also a lag effect in the development of businesses due to lower income levels of African Americans and the subsequent longer time frame needed to accumulate capital. Ong concluded that "although these businesses account for only a small fraction of the total business community, they demonstrate that if given the backing minority firms can operate profitably in new markets" (1982, p. 318).

Handy and Swinton (1983, 1984) did a longitudinal study of the variations in the rate of growth of African-American business sectors in different SMSAs between 1972 and 1977. Growth was defined as the number of firms, amount of receipts, and number of paid employees. The researchers found substantial variability from one SMSA to the next. This study showed that both market demand and resource availability were important factors influencing the rate of growth.

As market demand increased, both growth in the number of firms and in receipts increased significantly. The most significant demand factor associated with increasing receipts was growth of African-American consumer purchasing power. Growth of the local economy and growth of the African-American consumer market were the most important factors affecting the number of firms. Conversely, the general economic decline in African-American consumer markets in north central and northeastern SMSAs had a significantly negative impact on the rate of growth.

Similar to the previous studies, Handy and Swinton's (1983, 1984) research also found that the availability of financial capital was a significant factor in the growth of businesses. The level of capital provided by SBA and by African-American banks was a strong, significant determinant of business growth. In addition, the change in capital provided by SBA was a positive factor in increasing receipt growth. Although the initial level of SBA loan activity was not a significant factor in firm growth, the change in the level of funding was a significant factor in firm growth for SMSAs outside the South.

A particularly important finding was that both the level and change in the availability of professional and managerial manpower—African Americans holding professional and managerial positions in mainstream business firms—were important positive factors for growth.

A more recent study by Bates (1989) made use of the Characteristics of Business Owners (CBO) survey. This survey was conducted with a sample of the respondents to the 1982 Survey of Minority-Owned Business Enterprises. The CBO database provides much more detail on the demographic, human capital, and financial characteristics of business owners and their businesses.

Bates espoused a theory of inner-city economic development based on (a) interactions between characteristics of the inner city and the broader economy that may hinder economic development in the former and (b) the role that minority businesses might assume in improving inner-city economic development. Similar to proponents of the underdeveloped nation model, he argued that the inner city suffers from outflows of financial capital such as savings, income, and human capital. This condition is worsened by weak inflows. He stated that the retention of local entrepreneurs is a prerequisite for increasing the inflows of resources.

Bates tested his hypotheses by estimating econometric models for data on African-American and nonminority businesses. He examined the viability of firms that were established or entered between 1976 and 1982. He found that well educated business owners who employed large financial capital inputs were more likely to form viable businesses than those who were poorly educated with limited capital. Furthermore, he found that African Americans possessed fewer of the inputs associated with business viability.

Much of the previous research on African-American businesses had found that financial capital investment was an important determinant of business success (Ando, 1986; Bates, 1989; Handy & Swinton, 1983,1984; Ong, 1982). Bates (1993) found that initial capital investment was the single most important determinant of total receipts and survival.

Research has also shown that African-American businesses were more likely to experience discrimination by financial institutions (Chen & Cole, 1988). Bates (1993) compared African-American businesses to nonminority-owned (i.e., white male) firms and showed that African-American owners were less likely to receive loans. Those who were able to borrow received substantially smaller loans than nonminorities. When age, education, and equity capital were held constant, banks provided nonminority business owners with $1.83 in debt per dollar of equity while providing African Americans with only $1.16. Ando (1988) controlled for the firm's credit rating, size, and industry as well as the owner's equity investment, business experience and previous business bankruptcy or failure. She found that African Americans were much less likely to receive commercial loans than any other group.

Compounding the problem of apparent discrimination in lending based on a business owner's race is the practice of redlining minority neighborhoods. Redlining occurs when lenders provide fewer and smaller loans to businesses in minority neighborhoods. Bates (1993) found that redlining was being practiced against minority neighborhoods regardless of their location within the inner city or in affluent minority suburbs.

He concluded that lack of access to financial capital is an important barrier to the success of small African-American-owned firms. His findings provide empirical support for the conventional wisdom of proponents of the Black Capitalism model—African-American businesses suffer from a lack of access to capital and credit at reasonable rates.

The policy implications of these findings were made evident in April 1995 when the Comptroller of the Currency, the Office of Thrift Supervision, and the Federal Reserve Board published final rules for the Community Reinvestment Act (Community Reinvestment Act Regulations, 1995). Under the new regulations, banks will be graded on their performance in lending, serving (i.e., opening branches), and investing in poor or minority neighborhoods (*Statement of Eugene A. Ludwig,* 1995). In addition to disclosing their records on home mortgage lending, which is already required, banks would be required to provide information on consumer and small business loans. Banks that receive low grades can be fined or required to make improvements. These regulations apply to all state and federally chartered banks and savings and loan institutions.

Limitations of Previous Research

Two essential limitations on the previous research exist. For the most part, the analyses are done for African-American businesses in the aggregate. In addition, the impact of local economic variables is not always factored into the analyses.

Aggregate Analysis

Most of the previous research on African-American firms has analyzed these businesses as a whole. However, what applies in the aggregate may not hold true for subgroups. One way to disaggregate these businesses is by industry.

Two studies did attempt to disaggregate by industry. Simms and Burbridge (1986) investigated minority formation and failure within industries. Using the Standard Industrial Classification (SIC) level-two industry groups as the unit of analysis, they measured the impact of industry characteristics on the rates of minority business formation and failure. The industries Simms and Burbridge analyzed were construction, manufacturing, retail, transportation, nonprofessional, and nonfinance service businesses. The industry characteristics examined included capital-labor ratio, company size, and growth in employment and profit between 1972 and 1977. Due to data limitations, professional services and finance, insurance, and real estate (FIRE) were excluded. The authors recommended that further research be done on these industries.

For the industries included in Simms and Burbridge's analysis, financial capital intensity did not have a significant impact on failure rates of African-American firms. However, these researchers concluded that it was unlikely that this variable was unimportant and that further analysis was needed.

A second study examined a single industry. Grown and Bates (1992) analyzed variations in African-American business viability within the construction industry. Consistent with Bates' work on firms in the aggregate, they found that the most important determinant of survival was initial capital investment. However, a surprising finding was that unlike Bates' other research, education was not an important determinant of survival. Instead, employment history was a better predictor of survival for construction firms. This study indicates that factors significantly related to success may not be the same for each industry.

Additional evidence that different factors may be important to the success of different industries is provided by summary data on the growth in the number of minority-owned firms by industry. Between 1960 and 1980, manufacturing grew by 46% and wholesale by 111% (Bates, 1993). Firms in the business service sector and FIRE have experienced very rapid growth rates of 175% and 186% respectively.

It is reasonable to expect that the initial financial capital investment, or start-up capital, will be important to the success of some industries. For example, manufacturing firms typically require the purchase of equipment, parts, and supplies. Wholesale involves an investment in inventory. Both industries generally require a building or a substantial amount of space to house their operations. Each of these inputs costs money. These industries are financial capital intensive.

On the other hand, industries such as professional service and FIRE rely on the knowledge and skill of individuals. For example, consultants do not need to make an initial investment in equipment or a building in order to provide their service. Their essential inputs appear to be education and experience. These businesses are more likely to be human capital intensive. For them, start-up capital may not be significantly related to firm viability. This may explain the ability of these businesses to sustain very rapid growth despite barriers in accessing financial capital.

If education is a critical input for professional services and FIRE industries, one would expect an increase in access to education to have accompanied the growth in these firms during the period between 1960 and 1980. And indeed, high school dropout rates for 14- to 24-year-old African Americans declined from 21.6% in 1968 to 16% in 1980 (U.S. Bureau of the Census, 1981). By comparison, rates for whites fell slightly from 11.9% to 11.3%. The median number of school years completed by African Americans increased from 8.0 in 1960 to 12.0 by 1980. For whites the increase was from 10.9 to 12.5 years. The percentage of African Americans completing four or more years of college rose from 3.1% to 7.9%. For whites the rate increased from 8.1% to 17.8%. By 1975, the probability of college entry by those just completing high school was almost equal for African Americans (32.5%) and whites (33%) (U.S. Bureau of the Census, 1992b).[3]

In addition to education, managerial experience may be important to the viability of professional services and FIRE industries for two reasons. First, individuals who have been given managerial responsibility in other businesses or organizations have demonstrated a level of expertise worthy of attaining such positions. As managers they have had time to hone skills useful for operating their own businesses. Such skills may include developing networks with others in their field, organizing and prioritizing work, establishing and meeting schedules, negotiating, handling budgets, and supervising staff.

Second, Jovanovic asserts that individuals are uncertain of their managerial skill at the point of business start-up (Bates, 1989; 1990; and

1993). They increase their knowledge of their skill over time. Those who perceive that they are skilled will expand their businesses while those who believe they lack managerial skill will reduce or discontinue their firms.

Individuals who are managers in firms owned by others and believe they are skilled but have limited opportunities for further advancement may choose to start their own businesses. Managers who do not believe they have exceptional managerial skills will probably remain employees. Following this logic, business owners who have managerial experience prior to start-up should have a good sense of their ability at the point they enter business. This awareness should allow them to make good business decisions earlier than those without managerial experience.

Previous research on managerial experience has shown mixed results when African-American firms were analyzed in the aggregate. Handy and Swinton (1983, 1984) found that the level and change in the number of African-American professionals and managers working in private industry were significantly related to growth in the number of firms and the total receipts of African-American-owned businesses. Also, change in the number of professionals and managers was positively and significantly related to growth in the number of firms with paid employees. However, when Bates (1993) measured the impact of managerial experience of business owners on the receipts and survival of firms, he did not find a significant relationship. This lack of a relationship may be a result of the aggregate analysis. If managerial experience is a significant determinant of success for professional services and FIRE industries, it may have been suppressed when firms were combined across industries.

It is reasonable to think that prior managerial experience may benefit both wholesale and manufacturing industries as well as professional services and FIRE. However, an individual in one of the latter two industries may be able to establish a business based largely on managerial experience. An owner of a wholesale or manufacturing firm will still need to invest a substantial amount of money to get a business off the ground. Finally, managerial experience may be a determinant of loan amounts for firms that need financial capital. Bates' (1993) analysis of African-American firms in the aggregate found that this variable was not significantly related to loan amount. This study will further examine the impact of managerial experience.

Regional Economic Factors

The second limitation of previous research is that it has not always factored into the analysis the impact of regional economic determinants on the success of African-American-owned businesses. Bates (1993) did not include these factors in his model. However, some studies did. Handy and Swinton (1983, 1984) examined the impact of unemployment, per capita income, and the median family income of African Americans by SMSA. Their research showed that the change in unemployment and the level of African-American income were significantly related to growth in receipts. The change in per capita income was positively and significantly related to growth in the number of firms. Simms and Burbridge (1986) found that SMSAs with higher percentages of minority populations and declining unemployment rates had significantly lower failure rates among African-American owned firms. They looked at a sample of counties and found that the percentage of the population that is African-American is positively associated with survival.

Regional economic factors, such as the employment rate, may be indicators of both supply and demand effects. Banks in an area experiencing growth may be more inclined to make loans to businesses. High employment rates would indicate increased ability to accumulate risk capital and equity to leverage loans. These occurrences may increase the supply of businesses. High employment rates may also impact demand by enhancing the purchasing power of potential customers.

Expansion on Previous Research

This book expands upon Bates' (1993) previous work by (a) analyzing African-American businesses by industry and by (b) examining the impact of regional economic status on firm survival.

For the purpose of comparison, nonminority-male businesses will also be analyzed. The intent is to determine whether differences exist in the viability of African-American and nonminority businesses and, if so, whether they may be due to differences in the industrial or regional concentration of African-American and nonminority firms. If, for example,

African-American firms are found to be less viable, this might be due to excessive concentration of these firms in industries or regions that are in decline.

This study also assesses whether African-American and nonminority-male firms differ in the factors that are significantly related to viability. For instance, Grown and Bates (1992) found that education was not significantly related to the survival of African-American construction businesses; however, it was for nonminority firms. Such differences may have policy implications.

Notes

1. In addition 1,000 firms had $500,000 to $1 million in sales; 4,300 firms had sales of $200,000 to $500,000; 7,500 firms had sales of $100,000 to $200,000; 14,700 firms had sales of $50,000 to $100,000; 23,000 had sales of $25,000 to $50,000; 43,000 firms had sales of $10,000 to $25,000; and 41,000 firms had sales of $5,000 to $10,000. The top three industries which had the greatest number of firms with sales in excess of $1 million were retail trade, wholesale trade, and manufacturing.

2. Thirty-five percent of these employers were in retailing, 31% were in other services, 16% were in manufacturing and wholesale, 10% in construction services, and 8% were in professional services. The mean number of jobs per firm created by SBA loans was 16.9 in contracting services, 13.1 in manufacturing and wholesale, 8.7 in professional services, 6.9 in other services, and 5.9 in retailing.

3. The rate for African Americans began declining after 1975. This includes two-year and four-year colleges.

IV
Methodology

This chapter presents a detailed description of the research undertaken. An overview is provided followed by a description of the research questions, target population, and source of data. The data analysis section is presented with a discussion of the types of analyses conducted, the hypotheses involved, and the models used.

Overview

As previously stated, this study analyzed African-American and nonminority-male firms by industry. The industries analyzed in this research include the SIC major industry groups of manufacturing, wholesale, and FIRE. In addition, a professional services group was created by combining health, legal, educational, and social services from the SIC services group.

These are growth industries and emerging fields for African Americans, who have had only minimal participation in them in the past (Bates, 1993; Simms & Burbridge, 1986). Businesses in these divisions have shown substantially greater potential than those in the traditional, personal service fields such as "mom and pop" food stores, restaurants, laundries, auto service and repair, barber shops, and beauty salons. The emerging businesses are more likely to have owners with college degrees, much higher annual sales, paid employees, and a racially diverse clientele. They are also more likely to sell to other businesses and the government than traditional businesses.

Professional services and FIRE industries were regarded as human capital intensive, while manufacturing and wholesale firms were expected to be less so.

Research Questions

The research questions were as follows:
- Is start-up capital (i.e., the initial financial capital investment) significantly related to viability for different industries?
- Is education significantly related to viability for different industries?
- Is managerial experience significantly related to viability for different industries?
- Is the regional economy significantly related to the viability of different industries?
- Is industry decline or growth associated with business viability?
- Do African-American and nonminority-male businesses differ in their viability?
- How do African-American firms in professional services and FIRE industries compare with nonminority firms regarding factors related to viability?
- How do African-American firms in wholesale and manufacturing compare with nonminority firms regarding factors related to viability?

Target Population

The target population consisted of small African-American and nonminority-male owned businesses for which one of the following Internal Revenue Service (IRS) forms were filed: 1040 Schedule C (sole proprietorship); 1065 (partnerships); or 1120S (Subchapter S corporations). The target population was further limited to businesses that had sales of $5,000 or more per year. This last requirement excluded individuals who completed tax forms but may have conducted few or no business transactions (Bates, 1986).

Data Source

The primary source of data was the 1987 CBO database compiled by the US Bureau of the Census in 1991 (Nucci, 1992). The database contained information on five panels of business owners, including Hispanic, other minority (primarily Asian), female (both minority and nonminority), African-American, and nonminority-male. This study examined data from the African-American panel. The nonminority panel was analyzed for comparison purposes. The sample was drawn from IRS tax returns for businesses operating in 1987. Businesses were selected randomly within strata defined by panel, industry, geography, and size of firm (Nucci, 1992). All owners of each selected business were mailed a CBO questionnaire in 1991. Questionnaires were mailed to 127,600 business owners; 70% responded, yielding information on 89,000 business owners and 65,000 businesses.

The CBO survey provided (a) information on the owners' demographic (e.g., age and marital status), human capital, and financial capital characteristics as well as (b) data on the geographic location, financial status, and clientele of the business. The database was supplemented with IRS and Social Security Administration information on receipts, employment, SIC code, and the gender and ethnicity of firm ownership. This nationwide database is unique for its large size and because it contains information on the characteristics of both the owners and the businesses.

The operational definitions of variables from this database were consistent with Bates' variables because he also used a CBO survey as the data source for his study conducted in 1986 with owners of businesses operating in 1982.

Data Analysis

Bates (1993) analyzed the success of small African-American-owned businesses using survival from 1982 to 1986 as a dependent variable. The model he tested is presented below. The variable definitions and values are provided in Appendix A. The model is as follows:

Survival = f (Education, Management Experience, Owner's Age, Owner's Sex, Labor Input, Ongoing, Year of Start Up, Log Capital, Leverage[1])

In Bates' models, no further analysis was done by industry. The analysis in this book expanded upon Bates' work by conducting separate analyses by industry and region.

The variables used for this book were comparable to those used by Bates. They included the following:

- whether the firm survived from 1987 to 1991[2]
- log (real start-up capital)
- leverage
- whether the owner had a college degree
- hours the owner worked in the business in 1987
- whether the owner had managerial experience
- owner's age
- whether the owner was male
- whether the business was an existing one taken over by the owner or a new start
- whether the business was one year old or less in 1987

An additional variable used in this book, which was not used by Bates, was change in state employment from 1987 to 1991. This variable was a proxy for the regional economic status.

The variables of survival, college degree, managerial experience, gender, existing firm, and firm age of one year or less are dichotomous. The remaining variables, log (real capital), leverage, hours worked, and owner's age, are continuous.

The initial financial capital investment, i.e., start-up capital, was the measure of the amount of money invested at the time the owner entered the business. However, the years the businesses were started could differ by over 25 years from one firm to the next. Therefore, the value of the start-up capital across firms was not comparable. To gain comparability, the variable was converted to real 1987 dollars by dividing the start-up capital for each firm by the Gross Domestic Product deflator *(Economic Report of the President,* 1995) for the year the firm was started.

Univariate Analyses

Measures of central tendency and variance were conducted for African-American professional services, FIRE, wholesale, and manufacturing industries combined. The same was done for nonminority-male firms. The measures included the mean, standard deviation, median,[3] and interquartile range. These measures provided descriptive information about the data sets. They also allowed the comparison of results for two types of samples:

- The sample of all respondents, including observations which had responses on some variables in the model but not others and
- The reduced sample, which included only observations that had responses on every variable in the model.

The bivariate and multivariate analyses required the reduced sample. Therefore, it was informative to determine the similarity of the characteristics of the samples for these analyses and those of the full sample.

Univariate analysis was also used to examine the hypothesis that national growth rates of industries is a determinant of business viability. Descriptive data were used to determine whether differences in the survival rate of African-American and nonminority-male firms were related to concentration in particular industries. Data on the change in real gross domestic product by major industry group between 1987 and 1991 were compared with data on the distribution of firms across these industries by race.

Bivariate Analyses

These analyses were done to determine whether any significant relationships existed between the dependent variable and each independent variable when analyzed separately. (The results of these analyses are in Appendix B.) The data were aggregated across all four industries, and separate analyses were conducted for African-American firms and nonminority-male firms. The hypotheses for the bivariate analyses were as follows:

- Start-up capital is significantly related to survival.
- Leverage is significantly related to survival.
- Having a college degree is significantly related to survival.
- The number of hours worked in the business in 1987 is significantly related to survival.
- The owner's gender (for African-American firms) is significantly related to survival.
- Whether the firm was a new start or an existing business is significantly related to survival.
- Growth in state employment was significantly related to survival.

A simple logistic regression model was used rather than linear regression. When the dependent variable is dichotomous, such as firm survival, the response function forms an S-shaped or sigmoidal curve rather than a line, so a linear regression model was inappropriate (Neter, Wasserman, & Kutner, 1989). When the dependent variable can take on only two values, the error terms are nonnormal and the error variance is nonconstant.

The maximum likelihood estimation logistic function was used. The model for survival is presented below.

$$\ln (\Pi_i / 1 - \Pi_i) = \beta_0 + \beta_1 X_{i1} + E_i$$

Where

Π_i is the probability that $Y_i = 1$ for the ith firm

X_{i1} is the value of the independent variables of the ith firm

β_0 and β_1 are parameters

$i = 1, \ldots, n$

The independent variables of primary interest were log (real start-up capital), whether the owner had a college degree, and whether the owner had managerial experience. Based on the review of previous research, it appeared that these were the variables most likely to vary in their importance to firm survival when the firms were disaggregated by industry. Other independent variables in the model were leverage, hours worked in the business in 1987, owner's age, whether the owner was male, whether the business was an existing one taken over by the owner or a new start, and whether the business was one year old or less in 1987. This model was consistent with Bates'.

Multivariate Analyses

Multivariate analyses were used to determine whether there was a significant relationship between the dependent variable and each independent variable when all other independent variables in the model were controlled. The key hypotheses are stated below:

- The start-up capital is significantly related to the survival of firms in professional services and FIRE industries combined when all other variables are controlled.
- The owner's possession of a college degree is significantly related to the survival of firms in professional services and FIRE industries combined when all other variables are controlled.
- The owner's managerial experience is significantly related to the survival of firms in professional services and FIRE industries combined when all other variables are controlled.
- A regional economic factor, growth in state employment, is significantly related to the survival of firms in professional services and FIRE industries combined when all other variables are controlled.
- The start-up capital is significantly related to the survival of firms in wholesale and manufacturing industries combined when all other variables are controlled.
- The owner's possession of a college degree is significantly related to the survival of firms in wholesale and manufacturing industries combined when all other variables are controlled.
- The owner's managerial experience is significantly related to the survival of firms in wholesale and manufacturing industries combined when all other variables are controlled.
- A regional economic factor, growth in state employment, is significantly related to the survival of firms in wholesale and manufacturing industries combined when all other variables are controlled.

The maximum likelihood estimation for the multiple logistic function was used. The model for survival is presented below.

$$\ln (\Pi_i/1\text{-}\Pi_i) = \beta_0 + \beta_1 X_{i1} + \beta_2 X_2 + \ldots + \beta_9 X_{i9} + E_i$$

Where

Π_i is the probability that $Y_i = 1$ for the ith firm

$X_{i1}, X_{i2}, \ldots, X_{i9}$ are the values of the independent variables of the ith firm

$\beta_0, \beta_1, \beta_2, \ldots, \beta_9$ are parameters

$i = 1, \ldots, n$

A second logistic regression model was used to analyze the relationship between growth in state employment and firm survival. The model was created simply by adding a state employment variable to the model above. This regional economic variable was the growth in employment between 1987, the year about which most survey items were asked, and 1991, the year for which business survival was determined. The same analysis was conducted for nonminority-male businesses to examine whether the determinants of African-American business survival differed from mainstream firms.

The combination of professional services and FIRE industries was initially analyzed separately from the combination of wholesale and manufacturing because they were expected to differ substantially on several variables, particularly the barriers to survival. Running a single regression model with a variable distinguishing the industry group may not have captured the extent of the differences between the two groups. This was also the reason African-American firms were analyzed separately from nonminority-male firms. The models above were used for these regressions.

Two potential problems arose in analyzing the industries separately, as done above. If the variance in survival for one industry or group of industries differed from that of other industries, the results of the analyses may have been an artifact of the difference in the amount of variance there was to predict. Additionally, the effect of the variables of interest was allowed to change between industries. This change created an interaction term between the type of industry and each variable of interest.

To address this issue, a third logistic regression model was used to compare professional and FIRE industries with wholesale and manufacturing industries. An industry variable and three interaction variables were added to the model above. These independent variables were industry, the interaction between industry and college degree, the interaction between industry and managerial experience, and interaction between industry and start-up capital. The hypotheses associated with these variables were as follows:

- There is a stronger relationship between start-up capital and survival for professional service and FIRE industries combined than for wholesale and manufacturing industries combined.
- There is a stronger relationship between having a college degree and survival for professional service and FIRE industries combined than for wholesale and manufacturing industries combined.
- There is a stronger relationship between managerial experience and survival for professional service and FIRE industries combined than for wholesale and manufacturing industries combined.

Other Analyses

It would be desirable to conduct the multivariate analyses at a further level of disaggregation than professional and FIRE industries combined and wholesale and manufacturing industries combined. Each individual industry may have differed in the variables that were determinants of survival.

An attempt was made to further disaggregate the industries. Each of the four industries was analyzed separately. However, the number of observations for each industry was substantially reduced, especially the number of observations for nonsurviving firms for the dependent variable. The result was that the findings were much less reliable and have to be regarded with caution. These findings from the disaggregated analyses are presented in Appendix C.

Weighting

The 1987 Characteristics of Business survey sample is complex. It was stratified five ways, by (a) race, (b) gender, (c) major industry group, (d) state, and (e) receipt size class. Businesses were sampled disproportionately from these strata to ensure a sufficient number of particular types of firms for analysis (e.g., African-American firms). To address the problem of a nonrepresentative sample, the Bureau of the Census assigned weights to each observation. This weight was the reciprocal of the sampling fraction. These weights were then inflated to correct for nonresponse. A key assumption in this correction was that nonresponse would have been identical to the response values.

While weighting adjusted for the nonrepresentativeness of the complex sample, it created another problem. Once the sample had been weighted, analyzing it was like analyzing a census instead of a sample (Kalton, 1983; Kish, 1965; Lee, Forthofer, & Lorimer, 1989). When the number of observations is very large, the standard errors approach zero and lose meaning.

A technique called normweighting can be used to provide a technical correction for the problem. While this approach does not completely solve the problem, it is an accepted method used by other established researchers who have conducted and published research on this database. The formula for normweighting is to divide the sum of the weights by the mean weight. This reduces the weighted sample size to the actual sample size so that the standard errors can be defined. Normweighting was used in the analyses for this research.

Notes

1. Leverage is the ratio of debt to equity.
2. Firms which survived include those that remain open under the original owner and those that have been sold to a new owner and are still operating.
3. It should be noted that the medians had to be adjusted in order to prevent possible disclosures about individual firms. The method of adjustment was to use the mean of approximately 5% of the observations just above and just below the median.

V

Analysis of the Data

This chapter presents the results of the univariate and multivariate analyses. A discussion of the findings is then provided at the end of the chapter. The results of the bivariate analyses are presented in Appendix B.

Results

Univariate Analyses

Table 1 presents the number of firms (*N*), mean (*M*), standard deviation (*SD*), median (*Mdn*), and interquartile range (*Q3-Q1*) for the sample of all respondents for African-American firms in the professional services, FIRE, wholesale, and manufacturing industries combined. These measures are very similar to those in Table 2, which presents the same measures of central tendency and variance for the logistic sample. Over 70% of firms survived from 1987 to 1991. The financial variables showed that the mean amount of start-up capital for African-American firms across all four industries was about $31,000. The mean log of start-up capital was 6.5 and the leverage was about 2%.[1] Owners were 47 years old on average, over 50% graduated from college, about 30% had managerial experience, well over 50% were men, and they worked in their businesses full time. By and large, owners started new businesses rather than assuming ownership of existing firms. Less than 20% of the firms were one year old or less. State employment in the states where

Table 1. Univariate Analysis of African-American Sample with All
Respondents for Professional Services, FIRE, Wholesale, and
Manufacturing Industries Combined

Variable	N	M	SD	Mdn	$Q3-Q1$
		Continuous Variables			
Log (Real Capital)	2690	6.4641	4.3474	8.16	9.092
Real Capital	2690	30,819	183,483	3486.75	18,058
Leverage	2796	2.0029	5.3476	0	0.0471
Hours	2675	1976.42	1161	2064	1855
Owner Age	2767	47.0276	12.4996	49.5	20
State Employment	2796	-0.3859	2.7279	-1.54	3.69
		Dichotomous Variables			
Survival	2796	0.7076	0.4550	NA	NA
College Degree	2796	0.5381	0.4986	NA	NA
Managerial Exp.	2796	0.2888	0.4533	NA	NA
Male Owner	2796	0.5827	0.4932	NA	NA
Existing Firm	2796	0.0667	0.2496	NA	NA
Firm < 1 Yr	2796	0.1708	0.3764	NA	NA

Table 2. Univariate Analysis of African-American Logistic Sample for Professional Services, FIRE, Wholesale, and Manufacturing Industries Combined (N=2599)

Variable	*M*	*SD*	*Mdn*	*Q3-Q1*
		Continuous Variables		
Log (Real Capital)	6.5628	4.4474	8.16	9.092
Real Capital	31,650	19,4467	3,487	18,058
Leverage	2.1609	5.5182	0	0.0471
Hours Worked	2041.08	1156.47	2064	1625
Owner Age	46.6055	12.6368	49.5	20
State Employment	-0.3764	2.7676	-1.54	3.79
		Dichotomous Variables		
Survival	0.7707	0.4205	NA	NA
College Degree	0.5733	0.4947	NA	NA
Managerial Exp.	0.3225	0.4675	NA	NA
Male Owner	0.6270	0.4837	NA	NA
Existing Firm	0.0713	0.2573	NA	NA
Firm < 1 Year	0.1887	0.3913	NA	NA

these firms resided declined on average by about 0.38%, compared to an increase of 0.16% nationally (U.S. Bureau of the Census, 1989, 1992).

The univariate data for the sample of all respondents (Table 3) and the logistic sample (Table 4) for nonminority-male firms were also similar to each other. Over 80% of the firms survived. On average, real start-up capital was about $67,000, the log of real capital was 7.5, and leverage was about 2%. The owners had a mean age of 48, over 50% had college degrees, 40% had managerial experience, and 14% assumed ownership of an existing firm rather than starting a new one. Fourteen percent of the firms were one year old or less. State employment declined about 0.02% on average across the states where these firms resided.

It is interesting to note that African-American firms in the sample were established with one-half as much start-up capital as nonminority-male firms, but leverage was about the same for each group. The two groups were similar in the proportion of owners with college degrees. However, 9% more nonminority-male firms had owners with managerial experience than African-American firms. Slightly more African-American firms were one year old or less in age and state employment fell by 0.36% more in the states where these firms resided than in states where nonminority-male firms were located.

The findings showed that 6% more nonminority-male firms survived than African-American firms. The hypothesis was that the national growth rate of industries was a determinant of business viability. The question was whether differences in viability can be explained in part by differences between the concentration of the two groups in growing and declining industries.

Descriptive data were used to address this question. Table 5 shows the change in real gross domestic product by major industry groups between 1987 and 1991. Table 6 shows the distribution of African-American and nonminority-male firms across the major industry groups.

It is not clear, from comparing these two tables, that the difference in concentration between African-American and nonminority-male firms can explain their difference in survival. The percentage of nonminority-male firms in manufacturing was almost two times that of African-American firms, yet manufacturing was a declining industry. The percentage of nonminority-male firms in wholesale was three times that of African-American firms, but this was a no-growth industry. On the other

Table 3. Univariate Analysis of Nonminority-Male Sample with All Respondents for Professional Services, FIRE, Wholesale, and Manufacturing Industries Combined

Variable	N	M	SD	Mdn	Q3-Q1
		Continuous Variables			
Log (Real Capital)	4527	7.5198	4.3440	9.04	2.734
Real Capital	4527	66,921	317,117	8477.05	37,145
Leverage	5482	2.4452	5.8242	0	0.5872
Hours Worked	4517	2092.96	1073	2296	1548
Owner Age	4561	48.1559	12.9286	49.5	20
State Employment	4582	-0.0171	2.7809	-0.32	4.1
		Dichotomous Variables			
Survival	4582	0.8134	0.3896	NA	NA
College Degree	4582	0.5689	0.4953	NA	NA
Managerial Exp.	4582	0.4087	0.4917	NA	NA
Male Owner	4582	1.0000	0	NA	NA
Existing Firm	4582	0.1411	0.3481	NA	NA
Firm<1 Yr	4582	0.1358	0.3426	NA	NA

Table 4. Univariate Analysis of Nonminority-Male Logistic Sample for Professional Services, FIRE, Wholesale, and Manufacturing Industries Combined (N=4459)

Variable	M	SD	Mdn	Q3-Q1

Continuous Variables

Variable	M	SD	Mdn	Q3-Q1
Log (Real Capital)	7.5136	4.3881	9.05	2.734
Real Capital	66,755	322,476	8595.01	37,145
Leverage	2.4096	5.7468	0	0.59
Hours Worked	2101.53	1076.82	2296.2	1548
Owner Age	48.0725	12.805	49.5	20
State Employment	-0.0160	2.7660	-1.04	4.1

Dichotomous Variables

Variable	M	SD	Mdn	Q3-Q1
Survival	0.8322	0.3737	NA	NA
College Degree	0.5794	0.4937	NA	NA
Managerial Exp.	0.4135	0.4925	NA	NA
Male Owner	1.00000	0.0000	NA	NA
Existing Firm	0.1423	0.3494	NA	NA
Firm<1 year	0.1408	0.3479	NA	NA

Table 5. Real Gross Domestic Product by Industry as a Percentage of Real Gross Domestic Product, 1988 and 1991 (Percentage)

Major Industry Group	1987	1991	Difference
Gross Domestic Product	100.0	100.0	
Agriculture, Forestry & Fishing	1.9	2.0	+0.1
Mining	1.8	1.9	+0.1
Construction	4.7	4.0	-0.7
Manufacturing	19.3	18.7	-0.6
Transportation & Public Utilities	9.2	9.8	+0.6
Wholesale Trade	6.7	6.7	0.0
Retail Trade	9.7	9.8	+0.1
Finance, Insurance, & Real Estate	17.8	18.1	+0.3
Services	17.3	17.8	+0.5
Government	12.0	12.1	+0.1
Statistical Discrepancy Residual and Other	-0.5	-0.8	-0.3

Note. From "Gross Product by Industry, 1988-91" by Robert E. Yuskavage, November 1993, *Survey of Current Business,* p.41. Copyright 1993 by Economics and Statistics Administration, U.S. Department of Commerce. Although the title of the article refers only to years 1988-91, the articles also contained data for years prior to 1988.

Table 6. Distribution of Firms by Race and Industry (Percentage)

Industry	African-American	Nonminority-Male
Agriculture	1.64	2.85
Mining	0.00	0.74
Construction	10.52	17.83
Manufacturing	2.24	3.91
Transportation	10.75	5.36
Wholesale Trade	1.45	4.32
Retail Trade	16.24	15.76
FIRE	5.53	8.14
Services	46.51	36.50
Not Classified	5.13	4.58

hand, nonminority-male firms had a stronger presence than African-American firms in the FIRE industry, which was a growth industry.[2]

Given these mixed results, a conclusion cannot be drawn about the relationship between survival and concentration within growing or declining industries.

A second question was whether differences in survival between African-American and nonminority-male firms can be attributed to differences in regional concentration. The univariate analysis showed African-American firms were more heavily concentrated in states with employment rates which declined by more than rates in states where nonminority-male firms were concentrated. The multivariate analyses offered additional information on the relationship between state employment and firm survival.

Multivariate Analyses

This section presents the results of the multivariate analyses. Tables are provided with each of the independent variables and the dependent variable for the models discussed in Chapter 4. Tables 7 through 10 provide the variables for the model that is consistent with Bates' (1993) model. Tables 11 through 14 provide the variables for the model which was adjusted to include state employment. This latter model further expanded on Bates' work by examining the impact of a regional economic factor.

Only the results concerning the primary variables of concern—start-up capital, college degree, and managerial experience—are discussed in the "Results" section. The literature indicates that the importance of these three variables to firm survival may change based on the type of industry in which the firm is. The "Discussion" section, at the end of this chapter, will examine the results for some of the remaining independent variables that proved to be interesting.

As stated in the previous chapter, professional services and FIRE industries were combined and analyzed separately from the combined industries of wholesale and manufacturing. The central research questions were whether start-up capital, college degree, and managerial experience are significantly related to the survival of African-American firms when the industries are disaggregated in this way. In other words, will the results differ from those found by Bates when he examined African-American firms aggregated across all industries?

Wholesale and manufacturing industries. As expected, the results showed that for the sample of African-American firms in wholesale and manufacturing industries, start-up capital was significantly and positively related to firm survival when all other variables were controlled (Table 7). This means that the larger the initial financial investment made in these businesses, the more likely they were to survive. This finding is not surprising since the operation of these industries typically requires substantial investments in plants, equipment, and inventory.

The results also showed that the owner's possession of a college degree and managerial experience was significantly and positively related to the survival of businesses in these industries. Firms whose owners were college graduates appeared more likely to survive. Similarly, these wholesale and manufacturing businesses appeared to have a greater chance of survival if the owner had managerial experience.

For the sample of nonminority-male firms in the wholesale and manufacturing industries, start-up capital was also significantly and positively related to survival when all other variables were controlled (Table 8). The owner's possession of a college degree was not significantly related to survival. Managerial experience was significant, but was inversely related to survival. That is, firms with owners that had managerial experience appeared less likely to survive.

The results for African-American firms were consistent with Bates' findings for two of the variables discussed. Bates' research showed that start-up capital and education were significantly related to the survival of African-American firms aggregated across all industries. However, unlike the research in this book, he found that managerial experience was not significant for the aggregated firms.

Professional services and FIRE industries. Start-up capital was significantly and positively related to firm survival for the sample of African-American professional services and FIRE industries when all other variables were controlled (Table 9). This result was surprising since it was anticipated that these firms would be human capital intensive rather than financial capital intensive. The expectation was that these firms would survive, regardless of the level of start-up capital, if they had owners with college degrees and managerial experience. Yet the findings showed that

Table 7. Multiple Logistic Regression Analysis of African-American Firms in Wholesale and Manufacturing Industries Combined (N=1235)

Variable	Parameter Estimate	X^2	$p>X^2$
Log (Real Capital)	0.0577	10.5943	0.0011
Leverage	0.0045	0.1179	0.7314
College Degree	0.5618	7.3771	0.0066
Hours Worked	0.0003	27.2872	0.0001
Managerial Exp.	0.5638	7.0025	0.0081
Owner Age	0.0052	0.6423	0.4229
Male Owner	-0.2987	2.4884	0.1147
Existing Firm	0.2210	0.9451	0.3310
Firm < 1 Year	-1.0403	32.8099	0.0001

Table 8. Multiple Logistic Regression Analysis of Nonminority-Male Firms
in Wholesale and Manufacturing Industries Combined (N=2935)

Variable	Parameter Estimate	X^2	$p > X^2$
Log (Real Capital)	0.0631	24.6713	0.0001
Leverage	-0.0212	4.2942	0.0382
College Degree	0.1264	1.0628	0.3026
Hours Worked	0.0003	43.9197	0.0001
Managerial Exp.	-0.4191	12.4655	0.0004
Owner Age	0.0029	0.3951	0.5296
Male Owner			
Existing Firm	1.1914	30.2976	0.0001
Firm < 1 Year	-0.9480	53.1588	0.0001

Table 9. Multiple Logistic Regression Analysis of African-American Firms in Professional Services and FIRE Industries Combined (N=1364)

Variable	Parameter Estimate	X^2	$p>X^2$
Log (Real Capital)	0.1027	36.4895	0.0001
Leverage	0.0153	0.7568	0.3843
College Degree	0.3773	6.0584	0.0138
Hours Worked	0.0003	29.4379	0.0001
Managerial Exp.	-0.0214	0.0192	0.8899
Owner Age	0.0215	13.5519	0.0002
Male Owner	0.1002	0.4550	0.5000
Existing Firm	1.5051	6.8073	0.0091
Firm < 1 Year	-0.5940	12.2193	0.0005

start-up capital appeared to be necessary for the survival of these industries, just as with wholesale and manufacturing industries.

The results also indicated that the owner's possession of a college degree was significantly and positively related to the survival of these firms. As expected, the firms with owners who were college graduates were more likely to survive.

Contrary to expectation, managerial experience was not significantly related to the survival of professional services and FIRE industries. This finding will be discussed further in the "Discussion" section.

Table 10 presents the results for the sample of nonminority-male firms. With regard to start-up capital, the result was the same as for African-American firms. Start-up capital and managerial experience were significantly and positively related to the survival of professional services and FIRE industries when all other variables were controlled. Possession of a college degree was not significant.

The results were the same as Bates' (1993) results for the aggregate analysis of African-American firms. He also found that start-up capital and education were significant, while managerial experience was not.

The discussion of the multivariate analyses up to this point has been based on a model like Bates'. It was important that the models be consistent so that differences between the results of this research and that of Bates could be attributed to the analysis by industry and not to changes in the model. The next section will add state employment as a variable to the model to determine whether Bates' model can be improved upon by adding a local economic factor.

Growth in state employment for wholesale and manufacturing industries. To determine the relationship between regional economic factors and firm survival, the variable growth in state employment was added to the models for African-American and nonminority-male wholesale and manufacturing industries. Tables 11 and 12 present the results of the regression analyses for African-American and nonminority-male firms after state employment was added to the model. This variable was not significantly related to the survival of African-American owned firms when all other variables were controlled. It was significantly and negatively related to the survival of nonminority-male firms.

Table 10. Multiple Logistic Regression Analysis of Nonminority-Male Firms in Professional Services and FIRE Industries Combined (N=1524)

Variable	Parameter Estimate	X^2	$p>X^2$
Log (Real Capital)	0.1036	36.3284	0.0001
Leverage	0.0242	1.7534	0.1855
College Degree	0.0352	0.0469	0.8285
Hours Worked	0.0005	53.7298	0.0001
Managerial Exp.	0.3812	5.8290	0.0158
Owner Age	0.0008	0.0161	0.8990
Male Owner			
Existing Firm	1.6486	13.3687	0.0003
Firm < 1 Year	-0.8035	14.7580	0.0001

Table 11. Multiple Logistic Regression Analysis of African-American Firms in Wholesale and Manufacturing Industries Combined, with Growth in State Employment (N=1235)

Variable	Parameter Estimate	X^2	p>X^2
Log (Real Capital)	0.0596	11.2306	0.0008
Leverage	0.0020	0.0233	0.8787
College Degree	0.5887	7.9874	0.0047
Hours Worked	0.0003	28.0153	0.0001
Managerial Exp.	0.5945	7.6852	0.0056
Owner Age	0.0051	0.6307	0.4271
Male Owner	-0.3068	2.6215	0.1054
Existing Firm	0.2208	0.9359	0.3333
Firm < 1 Year	-1.0528	33.3558	0.0001
State Employment	-0.0383	1.9937	0.1580

Table 12. Multiple Logistic Regression Analysis of Nonminority-Male Firms in Wholesale and Manufacturing Industries Combined, with Growth in State Employment (N=2935)

Variable	Parameter Estimate	X^2	$p>X^2$
Log (Real Capital)	0.0615	23.2717	0.0001
Leverage	-0.0199	3.7820	0.0518
College Degree	0.0703	0.3252	0.5685
Hours Worked	0.0003	44.2075	0.0001
Managerial Exp.	-0.4425	13.8989	0.0002
Owner Age	0.0017	0.1313	0.7171
Male Owner			
Existing Firm	1.2202	31.5549	0.0001
Firm < 1 Year	-1.0191	59.6454	0.0001
State Employment	-0.0730	13.2763	0.0003

Growth in state employment for professional services and FIRE industries. The results for professional services and FIRE industries were similar to those for wholesale and manufacturing (Tables 13 and 14). Growth in state employment was not significantly related to the survival of the sample of African-American firms when all other variables were controlled. It was significantly and positively related to the survival of nonminority-male firms.

The "Discussion" section further addresses the results regarding state employment.

Analysis of interaction variables. Table 15 provides the results of the analysis when the industry variable and three interaction variables were added to the regression model for the sample of African-American firms. The results showed that the interaction between industry and start-up capital was not significant when all other variables were controlled. This means that one cannot be reasonably certain that the relationship between survival and start-up capital is any stronger for wholesale and manufacturing industries combined than it is for professional services and FIRE combined.

The same lack of certainty holds true for the interaction between industry and college degree and between industry and managerial experience. It cannot be concluded that the relationships between survival and these human capital variables are any stronger for professional services and FIRE industries combined than for wholesale and manufacturing industries combined.

The results for the sample of nonminority-male firms are provided in Table 16. The interaction between industry and start-up capital was significant and negative. The interaction between industry and college degree was not significant and the interaction between industry and managerial experience was significant and negative.

Discussion

Some of the findings are consistent with the expected outcomes; others are not. As expected, start-up capital is significant for African-American wholesale and manufacturing industries in the sample. Contrary to expectation, start-up capital is also significant for professional services

Table 13. Multiple Logistic Regression Analysis of African-American Firms in Professional Services and FIRE Industries Combined, with Growth in State Employment (N=1364)

Variable	Parameter Estimate	X^2	$p>X^2$
Log (Real Capital)	0.1029	36.5811	0.0001
Leverage	0.0146	0.6899	0.4062
College Degree	0.3738	5.9308	0.0149
Hours Worked	0.0004	29.6225	0.0001
Managerial Exp.	-0.0217	0.0197	0.8884
Owner Age	0.0213	13.2770	0.0003
Male Owner	0.0950	0.4080	0.5230
Existing Firm	1.4999	6.7772	0.0092
Firm < 1 Year	-0.5985	12.3926	0.0004
State Employment	0.0188	0.5242	0.4690

Table 14. Multiple Logistic Regression Analysis of Nonminority-Male Firms in Professional Service and FIRE Industries Combined, with Growth in State Employment (N=1524)

Variable	Parameter Estimate	X^2	$p>X^2$
Log (Real Capital)	0.1041	36.4424	0.0001
Leverage	0.0204	1.2525	0.2631
College Degree	0.0723	0.1960	0.6579
Hours Worked	0.0005	53.8394	0.0001
Managerial Exp.	0.3911	6.0911	0.0136
Owner Age	0.0022	0.1294	0.7190
Male Owner			
Existing Firm	1.6103	12.7203	0.0004
Firm < 1 Year	-0.7829	13.8372	0.0002
State Employment	0.0681	6.1201	0.0134

Table 15. Multiple Logistic Regression Analysis of African-American Firms Comparing Professional Services and FIRE Industries Combined with Wholesale and Manufacturing Industries Combined (N=2599)

Variable	Parameter Estimate	X^2	$p>X^2$
Log (Real Capital)	0.1074	63.7052	0.0001
Leverage	0.0111	0.9400	0.3323
College Degree	0.3510	8.0485	0.0046
Hours Worked	0.0003	57.1043	0.0001
Managerial Exp.	0.0084	0.0045	0.9464
Owner Age	0.0168	15.5859	0.0001
Male Owner	0.0347	0.0990	0.7531
Existing Firm	0.7811	8.8691	0.0029
Firm < 1 Year	-0.6764	30.1563	0.0001
Industry	0.2509	1.1881	0.2757
Industry & College	0.3364	1.0963	0.2951
Industry & Manage. Exp.	0.5280	2.4408	0.1182
Industry & Capital	-0.0551	3.7604	0.0525

Table 16. Multiple Logistic Regression Analysis of Nonminority-Male Firms Comparing Professional Services and FIRE Industries Combined with Wholesale and Manufacturing Industries Combined (N=4459)

Variable	Parameter Estimate	X^2	$p>X^2$
Log (Real Capital)	0.1119	88.6395	0.0001
Leverage	0.0042	0.1951	0.6587
College Degree	0.0387	0.1138	0.7358
Hours Worked	0.0005	119.3830	0.0001
Managerial Exp.	0.3761	11.4259	0.0007
Owner Age	0.0004	0.0124	0.9112
Male Owner			
Existing Firm	1.4007	40.3894	0.0001
Firm < 1 Year	-0.8880	59.1686	0.0001
Industry	0.6758	12.9771	0.0003
Industry & College	0.0846	0.1666	0.6831
Industry & Manage. Exp.	-0.7685	14.7153	0.0001
Industry & Capital	-0.0603	8.5803	0.0034

and FIRE industries. Furthermore, it cannot be concluded that the relationship between survival and start-up capital is any stronger for wholesale and manufacturing firms than for professional services and FIRE. It appears to be an important component for both sets of industries. This is a key finding.

As with start-up capital, possession of a college degree is significant for both sets of industries for African-American firms in the sample. It was expected that having a college degree would have a stronger relationship to survival in professional services and FIRE industries than in wholesale and manufacturing, but the results do not support this thesis.

A possible explanation for this result is that African-American owners are substituting education for start-up capital in wholesale and manufacturing, given the discrimination they face in lending. Bates (1993) and Ando (1988) found that lending institutions provided fewer and smaller loans to African-American firms when other credit factors were controlled. The univariate analysis for the sample in this book shows that, in the aggregate, African-American firms have one-half as much start-up capital as nonminority-male firms. Yet, the two groups have the same proportion of owners who are college graduates.

Table 17 provides data on owners' level of education by race and industry. For most industries, African-American owners lag behind nonminority-male owners in the percentage with college degrees. However, wholesale firms, like FIRE, have comparable percentages of owners who have completed college. Perhaps African-American wholesale business owners are offsetting their limited access to start-up capital with their education.

Another indicator that substitution may be taking place is that the percentage of college graduates in the African-American population is considerably smaller than that of nonminority males. However, the proportion of college graduates among African-American owners of wholesale firms is similar to that of nonminority-male owners. As previously indicated, the average age of African-American and nonminority-male owners in 1987 was 47 and 48, respectively. The proportion of African-American college graduates between the ages of 40 and 49 in 1988 was only 6.9 (National Center for Education Statistics, 1988). (The data are not available for 1987.) The comparable percentage for nonminority males was 14.2 or two times the rate of African Americans.

Table 17. Percentage of Firms Having Owners with College Degree by Race and Industry (Percentage)

Industry	African-American	Nonminority-Male
Agriculture, Forestry, & Fisheries	16.55	25.58
Mining		42.09
Construction	10.18	15.31
Manufacturing	13.31	25.81
Transportation & Public Utilities	10.22	13.50
Wholesale Trade	33.51	35.27
Retail Trade	22.58	27.97
FIRE	51.38	50.05
Selected Services	34.69	51.12
Industries not Classified	26.39	39.48

Note. There were no observations for African-American firms in the mining industry. In this table, the selected services industry is not limited to professional services. Consequently, the percentage of college graduates is not as high as would be expected.

Therefore, African-American wholesale business owners are much better educated relative to the African-American population than are nonminority-male wholesale business owners relative to the nonminority-male population.

Managerial experience is not significant for African-American firms in professional services and FIRE industries; however, it is significant for wholesale and manufacturing industries. This is the opposite of what was expected. One explanation could be that managerial experience is more important for industries with paid employees. Wholesale and manufacturing firms may be more likely to have paid employees. It is important to note that when the interaction variables are added to the model, managerial experience is not more important for wholesale and manufacturing firms combined than for professional services and FIRE industries combined.

The relationship between state employment and survival is not significant for African-American firms in professional services and FIRE industries or in wholesale and manufacturing industries. For nonminority-male firms this variable is significant, but negative for both sets of industries. It is surprising that this variable is not significant for African-American firms since they are more likely to be located in states where employment fell by a greater percentage. Given that African-American firms were initiated with half the start-up capital of nonminority-male firms, it may be that the lack of capital diminishes the importance of state employment for these firms.

Another possible explanation is that small businesses are started as an alternative means of making a living when people are faced with unemployment. Perhaps any decline in the number of businesses as the economy worsened was offset by new businesses established by employees who faced unemployment. Clearly there is room for more research on regional economic factors and business survival.

Two other independent variables are of interest because they are consistently significant in each analysis. Firms that are one year old or less are less likely to survive, regardless of race or industry. This finding supports previous research.

The second variable is number of hours worked in the firm in 1987. The results show firms with owners that spend more time in their businesses are more likely to survive. Several reasons may explain this relationship. The most straight-forward interpretation is that owners who commit more hours to their businesses are better able to hone their expertise and learn more about the nature of their firms and what is required to run them successfully.

This finding has important implications for African-American firms. These firms have less start-up capital and may, as a result, have lower levels of profit. If this is the case, owners' ability to support themselves on income from the firm alone is reduced and, therefore, they may have to work outside of their businesses. This reduces the time available to commit to their firms and consequently reduces the likelihood that these firms will survive.

The univariate analysis shows that African-American owners work in their businesses about 40 hours a week. This is the equivalent of full time; therefore, it is unclear whether they do have other jobs, in addition to business ownership. Further research is required to determine whether, in fact, African-American business owners tend to have additional jobs.

Another interpretation is that owners working in their firms part time are sensitive to other job opportunities. Part-time business people may be more likely to leave self-employment than full-time owners. They may try out self- employment on a part-time basis to find out if it is worth leaving their status as employees for something else. If this interpretation is accurate, it is likely that their businesses would have to be quite profitable to lure them away from employee status. Otherwise, the opportunity costs for full-time participation in their firms would be great. Conversely, full-time owners may have invested more in their firms or have fewer job options. They may be less able to leave self-employment even if their businesses are not profitable.

While the implications of the relationship between hours worked and survival are of interest, further research on these variables is beyond the scope of this study and will need to be addressed by future studies.

Suggestions for Further Research

Room certainly exists for additional research on African-American firms when they are further disaggregated by industry. An attempt was made, for this study, to examine each of the four industries separately, but the limitation in the sample size did not allow for reliable results (see Appendix

C). Future studies which use larger databases may allow for this level of analysis.

Additional disaggregation is important since, for example, professional services may differ in the factors key to survival when analyzed separately from FIRE firms. Real estate businesses may require little initial financial investment. On the other hand, some professional service providers, such as dentists, may have substantial start-up costs for equipment.

A sufficiently large database will also allow for disaggregation within an industry. For example, some types of manufacturers are growing while other areas are declining. The factors important to the survival of each may differ.

Notes

1. The low value for leverage is due, in part, to the fact that most firms in the sample borrowed zero dollars from the bank. That is, relatively few firms borrowed money. Therefore, when the sum of money borrowed is added across all firms and divided by the total number of firms in the sample, the average value is small.

2. The service industry shown in the tables includes professional services and nonskilled services. This industry group does not provide a sufficiently disaggregated level of information to assess growth and concentration for professional services.

VI

Policy Recommendations

Contrary to the position espoused by some researchers, African Americans do have a strong tradition of entrepreneurship as a means of economic development. While African-American businesses are underrepresented in terms of numbers of firms, research shows that existing firms display considerable variation in viability. Firms in emerging fields are proving to be quite competitive.

The research in this book shows that for African-American firms in these emerging fields, start-up capital and education are consistently important to the survival of professional services and FIRE industries as well as wholesale and manufacturing industries. These findings support Bates' results. The type of industry does not make a difference in terms of the importance of these factors. Additionally, managerial experience is important to the viability of wholesale and manufacturing firms.

Given these findings, what public policies should be developed or strengthened to support African-American business? This chapter will address this question. A number of recommendations are made, including those which address each of the key variables of interest as well as those that address long-term and short-term solutions.

Start-Up Capital

As previously indicated, SBA has a number of programs for small and minority businesses. Research by Ando (1986) and by Handy and Swinton (1983, 1984) shows that the availability of loans from SBA is critical for African-American firms. However, most SBA programs do not fill the need for start-up capital. Without a supply of start-up capital, potential entrepreneurs may become discouraged and never establish what might have been thriving businesses. Three policies are recommended to improve the supply of such funds: improvement of the SSBIC program, support for securitization, and better use of the Community Reinvestment Act. These proposals are discussed below.

Specialized Small Business Investment Company Program

The Specialized Small Business Investment Company Program or SSBIC (which serves small minority businesses), has the potential to be a good source of start-up capital if revamped. As previously stated, this program was intended to provide venture capital for business start-up costs. However, much of the assistance actually being provided by these companies is in the form of long-term loans rather than investments.

In 1994, SBA took steps to improve the Small Business Investment Company Program (SBIC, which serves small nonminority firms, too) by licensing 37 new SBICs which held a considerable amount of private funding. No new SSBICs were licensed. Minority firms did not get the same infusion of potential venture capital received by SBICs.

One policy recommendation is for SBA to provide the same kind of support for SSBICs as was provided for SBICs. Additional licenses should be dispensed to companies that have the capacity to make start-up capital available for African-American entrepreneurs.

Securitization

A related recommendation is that support be given for the use of securitization as a method of developing sources of funds for start-up capital. Securitization is a financial technique used by the private sector whereby the repayments from several individual loans are pooled into a single stream of income and then sold to private investors (Williams, Adley & Company; Chemical Securities Inc.; State and Federal Associates, Inc., 1994). This technique was pioneered by the Federal National Mortgage Association (FNMA) in the 1970s and has been widely used for residential mortgages. FNMA is a stockholder-owned, government-backed entity which issues its own bonds and notes in the capital market. The money raised is then used to buy mortgages from mortgage companies. In this way, FNMA creates liquidity for mortgage lenders to make more loans.

Securitization is now being proposed by economic development experts as a vehicle to be used by economic development lenders to provide capital for minority-owned businesses (Williams, Adley & Company, et al., 1994). Currently, these lenders hold each business loan to maturity and use the periodic payments to finance new loans. Under securitization, they would pool loans that are performing well and sell the loan package with its stream of interest income to private investors such as insurance companies, public pension funds, and commercial banks.

Securitization has four advantages over total reliance on publicly funded business loan programs:

- Securitization accelerates the flow of income to the development lender. Instead of receiving repayment for loans over a period of years, the development lender can sell pooled loans for immediate income which can be used to make more loans.
- Securitization provides economic development lenders with a tremendous supply of private funds with which to finance loans. It is estimated that the demand of institutional investors such as insurance companies and pension funds for investments in small business-related securities may be over $10 billion annually.
- Securitization rewards performance by providing access to private capital for development lenders with records of good loan management and service. This does not mean that these lenders reject entrepreneurs who have been unsuccessful obtaining commercial bank loans. Unlike banks, development lenders have the time and expertise to work with entrepreneurs to prepare the necessary financial packages.
- This technique reduces reliance on public funds and thereby reduces the risk and vulnerability that may result from changes in the political climate.

While securitization places emphasis on private sources of capital for small and minority businesses, public policy initiatives could facilitate the implementation of this strategy. Securitization is an information-driven financing method. Investors want to know the performance history of loans. SBA and other lending institutions have made many loans to small businesses and have collected information on the number and value of the loans. However, data on how the loans have performed, that is the record of payment on the loans, have not been collected. One proposal is to develop a database for information on the performance of loans by SBA and other lending institutions which can be used by economic development lenders who choose to pool these loans and market them to an investor.

A second proposal is to create a government-sponsored enterprise for minority business securitization, similar to FNMA. This entity would purchase loans that have been made to small businesses by banks and other lending institutions, such as economic development lenders, allowing these institutions to make more loans.

Community Reinvestment Act

Another source of capital is through direct lending from banks. There already exists a federal policy which can be used to encourage banks and thrift institutions to provide start-up capital to African-American businesses—the Community Reinvestment Act (CRA).

In 1977, Congress passed the CRA to encourage banks and thrift institutions "to help meet the credit needs of their entire communities, including low- and moderate-income neighborhoods, consistent with safe and sound lending practices" (Community Reinvestment Act Regulations, 1995). New regulations, passed in April 1995, are intended to increase the effectiveness of the Act by emphasizing improving performance, reducing paperwork for financial institutions, and evaluating institutions using three tests: lending, investment, and services (*Statement of Eugene A. Ludwig*, 1995). These tests include loans to small businesses and community-development loans and investments.

Institutions are evaluated by federal regulators and receive ratings based on the three tests. Their ratings are made public to the community they serve. If they receive poor ratings, the community can protest and bring pressure to bear on these institutions to provide better service. States can refuse to allow these institutions to expand or open new branches, and in other ways penalize them (Bates, 1993).

The CRA can be used effectively at the community, state, and federal levels to persuade financial institutions to provide start-up capital to African-American firms. The federal government should ensure that states and local communities are aware of the new CRA regulations and of how to effectively use them. An advertising and marketing campaign could accomplish these goals. Such an expenditure would be a justifiable investment since CRA requires no other public or private subsidy.

Community Development Financial Institutions Fund

In 1993, President Clinton proposed the creation of the Community Development Financial Institutions (CDFI) Program to assist distressed urban and rural areas (*Budget of the United States Government, Fiscal Year 1998*, 1997). The fund was created in 1994 and was intended to expand the availability of credit and investment capital, as well as financial and other development services. Grants and other financial and technical assistance are made to alternative lenders, such as micro-enterprise loan funds and community development banks, credit unions, and venture capital funds. CDFI also provides money to traditional banks and thrift institutions that increase their lending in economically distressed areas. All of these lenders, in turn, decide which projects to finance.

The White House budget proposed to increase the CDFI fund from the $45 million allotted in fiscal year 1997 to $125 million in 1998, a 178% increase. Also contained in the budget is $100 million in non-refundable tax credits to be distributed to equity investors in community development banks and venture capital funds. Support and increased funding for this program by Congress are strongly recommended.

College Education

Enrollment of African Americans in college increased dramatically from 150,000 in 1960 to over one million in 1975 (Green, 1989). However, this trend stopped in 1975. Attrition of minorities from college has become a problem. Among the 1980 high school seniors who enrolled in college, 21% of white students attained at least a bachelor's degree by 1986, while only 10% of African-American students did. The result is that the gap between white and minority graduation rates in college is growing.

For African Americans who do graduate from college, data show that they major in business at the same rate as white students. Among African Americans at least 18 years of age who held a bachelor's or higher degree in 1990, 19.3% had degrees in the field of business and management (National Center for Education Statistics, 1994). The percent for whites was 18.4. The choice of business and management was second only to education for African Americans (25.1% of African American and 17.6% of white graduates had degrees in education).

African Americans demonstrate a clear interest in preparing themselves for a career in business. The role of public policy in education should be to facilitate the enrollment and graduation of African Americans from college. Several recommendations can foster their attainment of a college education. These include both long-term and short-term solutions.

Elementary and Secondary School

First, a long-term investment must be made in elementary and secondary education to better prepare students for college. African Americans continue to drop out of high school at higher rates than whites. For African Americans between the ages of 14 and 34, the high school dropout rate in 1993 was 12.5%, compared to 7.3% for whites (National Center for Education Statistics, 1994). If students are lost early on, the pool of students who may enroll in and graduate from college is reduced. Steps must be taken to ensure African Americans are receiving the quality of education, at early ages, that will maintain their interest in school and prepare them for college.

The Goals 2000 Educate America Act, enacted in 1994, is intended to do just that. This is a comprehensive plan to achieve educational excellence. The plan includes the pooling of local, state, and federal programs; professional development; parental involvement; and building partnerships with community members such as businessmen. School districts may obtain federal grants, through their states, for long-term planning and for implementing their plans.

However, in 1996, some members of Congress proposed to eliminate Goals 2000 as a cost-cutting measure to balance the federal budget. Such action would have been a short-term solution that would have resulted in a long-term economic dilemma. If Goals 2000 had been terminated, it is likely that, in the future, fewer children would be prepared for college. Consequently, fewer potential entrepreneurs would be prepared to engage in successful businesses. This measure did not pass, and the White House has proposed a 26% increase in the program for fiscal year 1998 (*Budget of the United States Government, Fiscal Year 1998*, 1997).

This proposed White House budget also contains increased funding for two education technology programs that should further prepare students for college. Based on the premise that education technology can expand learning opportunities for all students and improve their achievement levels, President Clinton espoused the goal of linking every school to the Internet by the year 2000. In February 1996, he called on both the public and private sectors to work jointly to ensure that all students are technologically literate and that they achieve skills in communication, math, science, and critical thinking. Two programs were funded in fiscal year 1997. The first program was the Technology Innovation Challenge Grant Program. The 1997 budget made available $24 million in federal matching funds to school-centered, public/private partnerships that develop creative ways of applying technology to classroom curriculums. The proposed 1998 budget would increase these funds by 32% to $75 million. The second program was the Technology Literacy Challenge Fund. The proposed 1998 budget of $425 million more than doubles the 1997 budget of $200 million. This program is slated to receive $2 billion over the next five years. Congressional support for both programs is strongly recommended.

Another recommendation for improving elementary and secondary education is for Congress to authorize and fund the demonstration and evaluation of an education voucher system. Vouchers can be used by low-income parents to send their children to private schools they could not otherwise afford. Among the private schools from which parents might choose are over 300 independent African-American schools nationwide (Rudd, 1995). These are private schools funded by the African-American community and operated by African-American educators. Most use an African-centric approach to education which includes African and African-American history, culture, and literature, in addition to the standard academic curriculum. Their goal is to instill in students self-pride, self-confidence, and an orientation toward high achievement. These schools may be a viable option for parents who believe that public schools are failing their children, along with parochial or other private schools that do not meet their children's needs.

Undoubtedly, such a demonstration will evoke heated debate about the impact on public schools and on desegregation. Regarding desegregation, many urban schools are already highly segregated. Often urban public schools are predominantly African-American, while white students attend suburban or private schools. The impact of a voucher system on public schools is unknown. Some proponents of vouchers claim that such a system will compel public schools to become more competitive to attract students. As a result, they may improve and better serve children. Opponents claim that vouchers will drain funds from public schools and make it difficult or impossible for them to serve the remaining students well. When so much is unknown, research through demonstrations and evaluations would help to fill the information void.

Business Mentor and Internship Programs

Public policy should also promote business internships at the secondary school level. Programs can be developed through partnerships between schools and businesses which allow students to "shadow" the entrepreneur at work. Students would receive credit for spending time with a businessperson to learn what is required to operate a business, as well as the types of courses and degrees they need to enter various fields. This type of exposure increases the relevance of classroom work, creates an effective form of guidance counseling, and perhaps initiates the idea that entrepreneurship may be a desirable career.

College Scholarships, Grants, and Loans

Public policy can also facilitate entry of African Americans into college by supporting programs which provide financial assistance. Among existing programs are the Pell Grants, Student Loan Guarantees, Direct Student Loans, and National Service Americorp. Congress has considered proposals to substantially reduce funds provided under each of these programs in order to balance the budget. Such action could only exacerbate the financial barrier to college entry that some African Americans face. These programs should be protected.

The White House budget for fiscal year 1998 emphasizes college grants and scholarships. Included among the proposals is an increase in the maximum Pell Grant award from $2,700 to $3,000. If passed, this would be the largest increase in two decades. In addition, two new financial assistance initiatives were proposed. The Hope Scholarship would allow eligible families to take a tuition tax credit of up to $1,500 for each student attending postsecondary education for the first two years of college. The other option is a tax deduction for postsecondary tuition and fees. This deduction can be up to $5,000 in 1997 and 1998, and $10,000 beginning in 1999.

The Supreme Court also took action in May 1995 that could result in increased financial difficulty for potential college students. The Court let stand a ruling by the Fourth Circuit Court of Appeals in *Podberesky v. Kirwan* (Thompson, 1995). The lower court had ruled that the University of Maryland's Benjamin Banneker Scholarships, used to increase the presence of African-American students on its campus, were illegal. That court further determined that past discrimination could not be a basis for a race-specific remedy. The Supreme Court's decision not to hear the University's appeal has important implications for many colleges across the country which have similar scholarship programs.

Despite the Supreme Court's lack of support for race-based scholarships, colleges and universities can still offer financial assistance to African-American students by developing place-based scholarships. Such funds can be awarded to students who reside in economically distressed communities. Public policy can foster such initiatives by offering tax or other incentives to institutions that take such action.

Communities, states, and the federal government can also use CRA as a bargaining tool to encourage financial institutions in predominantly African-American communities to make loans to college applicants and students who reside there.

Historically Black Colleges and Universities

Additionally, support for historically Black colleges and universities (HBCUs) should be expanded. These institutions have a tradition of creating rigorous academic programs as well as a supportive environment for African-American students. Consequently, these students are more likely to graduate if they attend HBCUs than if they attend white institutions. HBCUs enroll 18% of all African-American students, yet they awarded 34% of all baccalaureate degrees earned by African-Americans in 1984-85 (Green, 1989). This higher rate of graduation at HBCUs cannot be attributed to lower academic standards. Indeed, 75% of African-Americans who receive their master's and doctoral degrees from white institutions were undergraduates of HBCUs (Rudd, 1995). Clearly, HBCUs are graduating well-prepared students.

Currently, legislation exists which provides federal funding for Howard University, and the 1890 Morrill Act authorizes support for the African-American land grant colleges. However, Congress has periodically threatened to reduce the Howard University funds, and support for land grant colleges has been minimal. Not only should backing be shored up for these institutions, it should be expanded to the remaining HBCUs not currently receiving such support.

Diversity in White Colleges and Universities

The enrollment and graduation of African Americans can also be enhanced by increasing the diversity of predominantly white colleges and universities. However, in July 1995 the regents of the California Board of Regents, which governs the University of California system, voted to end admissions which take race or gender into consideration. This action was part of a broader initiative to end affirmative action in California that resulted in Proposition 209 being placed on the election ballot in November 1996. Voters passed this measure, which banned preferential treatment and discrimination in public hiring, contracting, and education. Opponents of Proposition 209 challenged it in court and won an injunction blocking the enforcement of the measure. However, this lower court ruling was overturned by the U.S. Circuit Court of Appeals, allowing implementation of the measure to move forward.

The action of the Board of Regents runs counter to the expressed position of Supreme Court Justice Powell, which strongly influenced the ruling in the *Regents of the University of California v. Bakke*. His written opinion argued that affirmative action is beneficial when it promotes a more inclusive and diverse society (Dellinger, 1995).

The American Council on Education supports increased diversity in colleges and universities and has developed a method for schools to accomplish this. It advocates that schools take a comprehensive approach including the following strategies:

- Develop a task force with broad representation to address the issue of diversity.
- Conduct an institutional audit which discerns the historical presence of minority students, faculty, and administrators at the institution.
- Develop a plan with goals, timetables, and an evaluation component.
- Allocate sufficient resources.
- Develop minority mentoring programs for students, faculty, and staff.

Public policy can encourage institutions to adopt these recommendations by providing them with incentives. Such incentives can take the form of eligibility for special tax benefits or funds for schools that undertake an initiative to diversify their campuses. These special funds could be used by the schools to help cover the cost of a diversity program.

Minority Business Development Agency

The MBDA has set forth a number of proposals in its *Research and Policy Report* (Fratoe, 1994) to encourage minority youth to prepare for careers as entrepreneurs. One proposal is for the Agency to affect the supply of "minority enterprise college scholarships [and] fellowships" (Recommendation #26).

One strategy for accomplishing this is for MBDA to work with banks and businesses that serve African-American communities. For example, banks could earn favorable ratings with respect to the Community Reinvestment Act by providing scholarships, fellowships, or very low-interest loans for college education to residents of the African-American communities they serve. Businesses could be given special recognition for the provision of scholarships and fellowships to students attending high school (and middle school) in African-American communities where these businesses operate.

The reduction in staffing and funding resources that MBDA sustained in 1996 limits the likelihood that it can carry out this work. It is recommended that the resources which were cut be restored so that this agency can continue to function effectively. It is the only federal agency created to promote the formation and growth of competitive, minority-owned businesses (Fratoe, 1995).

Negotiations on the fiscal year 1998 budget are underway in Congress as this book is being written. Thus, it is not known whether the funding levels proposed by the White House will be passed. If they are, then several of the programs discussed above, which would be funded for the first time or receive increased funding, may have a substantial impact on the number of African-American students who can enter college and graduate.

Managerial Experience

Managerial experience was found to be significantly related to the survival of wholesale and manufacturing firms. Therefore, some policy options which facilitate the acquisition of such experience and the entry of people with managerial experience into business are warranted.

Policy support for the acquisition of managerial experience can be achieved in several ways. First, public policy should provide incentives for businesses to create internship programs for African-American college students interested in business careers. These internships should be designed to expose students to what is required to manage a firm.

Second, public policy should be used to create an internship program for students just graduating from college. This program would be similar to the existing Presidential Management Internship Program that places graduates with interests in public administration in civil service jobs for two years so they can get the experience they need for their careers. Private sector placements should also be developed for these business interns. Tax and other incentives could be used to encourage businesses to hire graduates through this internship program.

Third, public policy should facilitate the movement of African Americans who are employed as managers into entrepreneurship. An increasing number of African Americans who work in corporations and who have found their upward mobility blocked are opting to leave and start their own firms:

... many black executives who find themselves stuck in middle management are quitting corporate life to become entrepreneurs. They want to call their own shots in business where color will not limit how high they rise or how much they earn ("Blacks Who Left Dead-End Jobs to Go it Alone," 1984, p. 104)

These executives also face the problem of securing enough start-up capital to make their ventures successful. Public policy should facilitate access to capital by making it easier for individuals with managerial experience to receive direct loans or loan guarantees. This could involve revisions to the SSBIC program so that economic development lenders have more incentive to make loans to people with management backgrounds. It could also involve the development of a new program which targets former managers for start-up loans and loan guarantees.

Policy Recommendations Concerning Other Variables in the Model

Start-up capital, college education, and managerial experience were the key variables of interest in this study. However, some of the other variables tested in the model were important to African-American firm survival and have policy implications as well. These include the age of the firm and the number of hours the owners worked in their businesses.

Firms One Year Old or Less

Firms that are less than a year old are least likely to survive. Public policy should provide special support for very young firms. The proposals for facilitating access to start-up capital should assist these firms. If they begin with sufficient financial resources, they should experience less trauma during the period when the owners are trying to establish their product or service in the market place. They should also be in a better position to cope with unforeseen expenses and emergencies.

In addition, new owners may benefit from technical assistance such as establishing an accounting system and handling tax payments and legal issues. The MBDCs across the country already provide such services. However, in most, if not all, instances, business owners are expected to go to the centers for assistance. Since new businesses are often one-person enterprises, obtaining technical assistance may, therefore, require owners to close their shops and risk losing business while they are gone. Public policy should address this obstacle by providing for on-site technical assistance by the MBDCs. Again, this will require that funding for MBDA be restored, at least to levels provided prior to the 1996 cuts.

Hours Worked

The findings from this study show that as the number of hours the owner works in the firm increases, so does the likelihood that the firm will survive. As previously discussed, however, owners who are unable to support themselves on the income from their businesses may be forced to work other jobs, thereby leaving them less time to devote to their own enterprises. These firms are more prone to fail. Recommendations discussed above which are intended to increase the availability of start-up capital can also assist these firms and their owners. The availability of such funds should relieve some of the economic burden faced by these owners and reduce their need for outside jobs.

Micro-Enterprise for Low-Income Entrepreneurs

The African Americans who are in the best position to take advantage of entrepreneurship as an option for economic development are those who already have some equity capital, a college education, and managerial experience. These potential entrepreneurs are more likely to be middle-class people, many of whom benefited from the civil rights movement and the increased opportunities to go to college, secure jobs with good salaries, and receive promotions. However, public policy can also support entrepreneurship as a means by which low-income people can achieve self-sufficiency. Support for micro-enterprise is one option.

Micro-enterprises are very small businesses, typically with less than five employees. From 1990 to 1992, the U.S. Department of Health and

Human Services (DHHS) funded a demonstration program designed to help low-income people in four states to start micro-businesses (DHHS, 1994). Grants were provided to community action agencies to establish or continue to run micro-enterprise programs. Participants were taught how to write business plans, make loan applications, and manage their new businesses. The participants included AFDC and food stamp recipients as well as the homeless and working poor. Of the 811 participants in the demonstration, 153 or nearly 19% started businesses.

These businesses encountered some of the same obstacles that have been investigated in this book. The primary concern expressed by participants in each of the four states was the lack of access to capital. This was considered a major barrier to business viability. Another important factor was insufficient long-term follow-up by the agencies offering the programs.

Public policy can support self-sufficiency for low-income people through the authorization of legislation which converts this demonstration project into a federal program. One component of the program would be to fund entities such as community-based organizations to provide the business training and follow-up support to individuals interested in starting businesses. A second component would be the creation of funds that can be used as start-up capital specifically for these micro-enterprises.

Block Grants

As part of the initiative to restructure government, many members of Congress currently advocate the use of block grants to provide publicly funded programs. Block granting is a strategy whereby lump sums of money are provided to the states to create their own programs within broad federal guidelines. These grants often involve a reduction in the total amount of funds made available for the programs over time. It is useful to consider how this strategy might affect minority business development.

Research findings from both this book and previous studies indicate that block granting could have a mixed effect on African-American business development. On the one hand, the research herein indicated that the local economic factor, state employment, is not significantly related to the survival of these businesses. This would suggest that local control may not be the answer to increasing the net number of successful African-American firms. On the other hand, Bates (1993) found that firms in locations with African-American elected officials benefited from programs intended to enhance the development of these firms. This suggests that in places where the local government is supportive of African-American business development, local control could be very beneficial. It could also be argued that in locations that are not supportive of this kind of development, barriers could be erected such as the use of the *Adarand Constructors, Inc. v. Peña* case to limit the use of minority business development programs.

On the whole, it appears that ending the federal administration for minority business development programs is not warranted. Under federal administration, locations that are not inclined to support these programs would have to meet at least the minimal federal requirement. Locations that are inclined to do more will do so.

Summary

There is a need to reduce the gap between the economic status of African-Americans and whites. Yet, recent legislation and current policy proposals to restructure government and reduce the federal budget threaten to worsen the economic well being of middle-class and working-class African Americans, as well as the poor.

One vehicle which can be used to create jobs and increase revenue for African-American communities is business ownership. This study demonstrates that African Americans have a long history of using business enterprise to achieve economic development and self-sufficiency.

African-American business ownership creates jobs and promotes economic development on several levels. Single proprietorships generate jobs for the owners and provide evidence to potential entrepreneurs that business ownership is a viable option. Firms with paid employees generate multiple jobs. African-American employers primarily hire other African Americans and are, therefore, an important source of employment. Finally, African-American firms may also generate jobs for other African-American firms with which they do business.

The research reported in this book adds to existing knowledge about the factors that contribute to the survival of African-American businesses. It was found that even when industries are disaggregated, start-up capital is still significantly related to the survival of firms in emerging fields. In addition, the possession of a college degree is consistently significant, and managerial experience is significant for firms in wholesale and manufacturing.

Based on these findings, public policy should a) support the development of start-up capital for entrepreneurs creating new businesses, b) facilitate African-American enrollment in and graduation from college, and c) create incentives for businesses to provide managerial experience to students and graduates, as well as incentives for existing managers to develop their own firms. Several policy proposals recently considered and legislation passed by Congress are inconsistent with the findings of this study and may exacerbate the disparity between the economic status of African Americans and whites.

Public policy is best designed when it is based on sound research rather than political whim, ambition, or expediency. This book offers a basis from which to generate effective public policy.

Appendix A
Bates' Variable Definitions

Bates' (1993) definition of the variables are provided below with an indication of changes necessitated by the use of the 1987 database rather than the 1982 database.

Independent Variables

Ed2:   For owners completing four years of high school, the value of Ed2 = 1; otherwise, Ed2 = 0.

Ed3:   For owners completing at least one but fewer than four years of college, the value of Ed3 = 1; otherwise, Ed3 = 0.

Ed4:   For owners completing four or more years of college, the value of Ed4 = 1; otherwise, Ed4 = 0.

Management: For owners who had worked in a managerial capacity prior to owning the business they owned in 1982, management = the number of years one had worked as a manager.

Age2:   For owners between the ages of 35 and 44, Age2 = 1; otherwise, Age2 = 0.

Age3:   For owners between the ages of 45 and 54, Age3 = 1; otherwise, Age3 = 0.

Age4:   For owners 55 or older, Age4 = 1; otherwise, Age4 = 0.

Sex: For male owners, Sex = 1; otherwise, Sex = 0.

Labor Input: The average number of hours per week in 1982 spent by
                           owners working in or managing the businesses that they
                           owned. Hours worked in 1987 was used for this book.

Ongoing: If the owner entered a business that was already in
                           operation, Ongoing = 1; if the owner founded the
                           business, then Ongoing = 0.

Time82:   If the business was started or ownership was acquired
                           during 1982, then Time82 = 1; otherwise, Time82 = 0.

Time80:   If the business was started or ownership was acquired
                           during 1980 or 1981, then Time80 = 1; otherwise,
                           Time80 = 0.

Log Capital: The logarithm of the sum of debt and equity capital.

Leverage: The ratio of debt to equity; the value of this ratio is
                           constrained not to exceed 19.

Debt: The borrowed money used to start or become an owner
                           of the business, measured in dollars.

Equity: The financial capital (other than borrowed money) used
                           to start or become an owner of the business. Assets
                           contributed by the owner at the point of business entry
                           were also included as equity.

Industry: A series of dummy variables which identify firms in six
                           major industry groups: a) construction, b) manufacture,
                           c) transportation (includes communication and public
                           utilities), d) trade (includes both wholesale and retail
                           industries), e) FIRE

Dependent Variables

Survival: Remaining in operation from 1982 to 1986.

Log Receipts: The logarithm of total receipt revenues for the 1982 calendar year.

Appendix B
Bivariate Analysis

Tables B1 and B2 show the results of the bivariate logistic analyses for African-American and nonminority-male firms, respectively. Data are provided on the parameter estimates, Chi Square values, and the probability of observing a value equal to or greater than Chi Square when the null hypothesis is true.

For African-American firms, all of the independent variables except state employment had values of X^2 with $p < .05$. Thus, the results support the hypotheses, with the exception of state employment. That is, one can be at least 95% certain that each of the independent variables except state employment is significantly related to survival. One cannot reasonably conclude that state employment is significantly related to survival since its X^2 value has a $p > .05$.

Table B-2 shows that the results for nonminority-males do not support the hypothesis that having a college degree is a determinant of survival. All other hypotheses are supported; that is, one can be at least 95% certain that each of the variables except college degree is a determinant of survival.

Table B1. Bivariate Logistic Regression Analyses of African-American Firms in Professional Service, FIRE, Wholesale, and Manufacturing Industries Combined (N=2599)

Variable	Parameter Estimate	X^2	$p>X^2$
Log (Real Capital)	0.1263	150.7202	0.0001
Leverage	0.0521	22.0241	0.0001
College Degree	0.4027	18.4581	0.0001
Hours Worked	0.00041	96.4500	0.0001
Managerial Exp.	0.3746	12.8727	0.0003
Owner Age	0.0214	31.3172	0.0001
Male Owner	0.5451	33.2135	0.0001
Existing Firm	1.0066	16.6884	0.0001
Firm < 1 Year	-1.1409	112.9385	0.0001
State Employment	0.0173	1.0453	0.3066

Table B2. Bivariate Logistic Regression Analyses of Nonminority-Male Firms in Professional Service, FIRE, Wholesale, and Manufacturing Industries Combined (N=2599)

Variable	Parameter Estimate	X^2	$p>X^2$
Log (Real Capital)	0.1377	257.2580	0.0001
Leverage	0.0529	31.1650	0.0001
College Degree	0.00264	0.0011	0.9740
Hours Worked	0.00056	223.4280	0.0001
Managerial Exp.	0.2973	12.7342	0.0004
Owner Age	0.00681	4.6619	0.0308
Male Owner			
Existing Firm	1.8037	70.9434	0.0001
Firm < 1 Year	-1.2677	175.9643	0.0001
State Employment	0.0450	9.4327	0.0021

Appendix C
Multiple Logistic Regression Analysis
by Individual Industry

Table C1 shows that start-up capital was significantly and positively related to survival for African-American firms in the professional services industry. College degree and managerial experience were not significant; thus, one cannot be reasonably certain that either is a determinant of survival.

Start-up capital and managerial experience for nonminority-males were positive and significant (Table C2). The hypothesis for each is supported. College degree was also significant, but negatively related to survival. Firms with owners who graduated from college were less likely to survive.

For African-American firms in the FIRE industry, start-up capital and college degree were positive and significant (Table C3). Managerial experience was also significant, but negative. Firms with owners who had managed before were less likely to survive.

Start-up capital for nonminority-male FIRE firms was positive and significant (Table C4). College degree and managerial experience were not significant; one cannot reasonably conclude that either is a determinant of survival.

Table C5 shows the results for African-American firms in the wholesale industry. Start-up capital and managerial experience were significant and positive for African-American firms in the wholesale industry. College degree was not significant; thus, one cannot reasonably conclude that it was a determinant of survival.

Start-up capital and managerial experience were both significant for nonminority-male firms in wholesale (Table C6). However, start-up capital

Table C1. Multiple Logistic Regression Analysis of African-American Firms in the Professional Services Industry (N=833)

Variable	Parameter Estimate	X^2	$p>X^2$
Log (Real Capital)	0.0913	17.5477	0.0001
Leverage	0.0006	0.0010	0.9754
College Degree	0.3378	2.2364	0.1348
Hours Worked	0.0003	14.9437	0.0001
Managerial Exp.	0.1945	0.9055	0.3413
Owner Age	0.0057	0.6684	0.4136
Male Owner	0.2716	1.8337	0.1757
Existing Firm	1.0427	3.0088	0.0828
Firm < 1 Year	-0.5405	5.9951	0.0143

Table C2. Multiple Logistic Regression Analysis of Nonminority-Male
Firms in the Professional Services Industry (N=723)

Variable	Parameter Estimate	X^2	$p>X^2$
Log (Real Capital)	0.1781	39.7174	0.0001
Leverage	0.0744	3.4319	0.0639
College Degree	-0.9136	5.5620	0.0184
Hours Worked	0.0006	26.2707	0.0001
Managerial Exp.	0.5357	4.5538	0.0328
Owner Age	-0.0284	9.1104	0.0025
Male Owner			
Existing Firm	2.1955	3.6441	0.0563
Firm < 1 Year	-1.1446	10.3475	0.0013

Table C3. Multiple Logistic Regression Analysis of African-American Firms in the FIRE Industry (N=531)

Variable	Parameter Estimate	X^2	$p>X^2$
Log (Real Capital)	0.1211	15.8002	0.0001
Leverage	0.1267	2.8772	0.0898
College Degree	0.5134	4.0471	0.0442
Hours Worked	0.0005	16.1235	0.0001
Managerial Exp.	-0.7470	7.5764	0.0059
Owner Age	0.0650	31.0108	0.0001
Male Owner	-0.2721	1.0503	0.3054
Existing Firm	5.4143	1.8962	0.1685
Firm < 1 Year	-0.9698	10.4847	0.0012

Table C4. Multiple Logistic Regression Analysis of Nonminority-Male Firms in the FIRE Industry (N=801)

Variable	Parameter Estimate	X^2	$p>X^2$
Log (Real Capital)	0.0567	6.2315	0.0125
Leverage	-0.0148	0.4609	0.4972
College Degree	0.2957	2.1045	0.1469
Hours Worked	0.0005	24.1577	0.0001
Managerial Exp.	0.1177	0.3066	0.5798
Owner Age	0.0277	9.5822	0.0020
Male Owner			
Existing Firm	1.6518	11.7477	0.0006
Firm < 1 Year	-0.7102	7.1136	0.0077

Table C5. Multiple Logistic Regression Analysis of African-American Firms in the Wholesale Industry (N=670)

Variable	Parameter Estimate	X^2	$p > X^2$
Log (Real Capital)	0.1118	22.1738	0.0001
Leverage	0.0182	0.7387	0.3901
College Degree	-0.1111	0.2238	0.6361
Hours Worked	0.0002	5.1508	0.0232
Managerial Exp.	0.5306	4.4214	0.0355
Owner Age	0.0114	1.4676	0.2257
Male Owner	-0.6547	6.0730	0.0137
Existing Firm	0.0773	0.0607	0.8054
Firm < 1 Year	-1.0090	19.6667	0.0001

Table C6. Multiple Logistic Regression Analysis of Nonminority-Male Firms in the Wholesale Industry (N=1619)

Variable	Parameter Estimate	X^2	$p>X^2$
Log (Real Capital)	0.0381	5.9775	0.0145
Leverage	-0.0136	0.7083	0.4000
College Degree	0.1387	0.9427	0.3316
Hours Worked	0.0003	23.0042	0.0001
Managerial Exp.	-0.6010	18.0215	0.0001
Owner Age	-0.0035	0.3557	0.5509
Male Owner			
Existing Firm	1.3145	22.5177	0.0001
Firm < 1 Year	-0.9088	30.4979	0.0001

was positively related to survival and managerial experience was inversely related. College degree was not significant.

Table C7 indicates, for the first time, that start-up capital for African-American firms, in this case manufacturing firms, was not significant. This is a surprising finding which may be due to the reduced sample size and decreased reliability. It may also be an indication that these firms are substituting education and managerial experience, which were both significant and positive, for start-up capital.

The last table (Table C8) shows that start-up capital was significant and positive for nonminority-male firms. Managerial experience was significant and negative and college degree was not significant.

Table C7. Multiple Logistic Regression Analysis of African-American Firms in the Manufacturing Industry (N=565)

Variable	Parameter Estimate	X^2	$p>X^2$
Log (Real Capital)	0.0137	0.2496	0.6173
Leverage	0.0041	0.0505	0.8221
College Degree	1.9132	13.0938	0.0003
Hours Worked	0.0005	23.9109	0.0001
Managerial Exp.	0.8423	4.6804	0.0305
Owner Age	-0.0068	0.5073	0.4763
Male Owner	0.0548	0.0364	0.8487
Existing Firm	0.2732	0.6312	0.4269
Firm < 1 Year	-0.9554	10.0142	0.0016

Table C8. Multiple Logistic Regression Analysis of Nonminority-Male
Firms in the Manufacturing Industry (N=1316)

Variable	Parameter Estimate	X^2	p>X^2
Log (Real Capital)	0.0846	12.9785	0.0003
Leverage	-0.0377	7.1222	0.0076
College Degree	-0.0592	0.0596	0.8072
Hours Worked	0.0004	20.3884	0.0001
Managerial Exp.	-0.7545	6.4673	0.0110
Owner Age	0.0141	3.4326	0.0639
Male Owner			
Existing Firm	0.9187	6.7030	0.0096
Firm < 1 Year	-0.9483	18.5942	0.0001

Bibliography

Adarand Constructors, Inc. v. Peña, 63 U.S.L.W. 4523 (U.S. June 12, 1995).

Allen, L. (1971). Making capitalism work in the ghettos. In R.W. Bailey (Ed.), *Black business enterprise* (pp.138-149). New York: Basic Books.

Allen, R.I. (1969). *Black awakening in capitalist America*. Garden City, NY: Doubleday & Company.

America, R.F., Jr. (1971). What do you people want. In R. W. Bailey (Ed.), *Black business enterprise* (pp. 124-137). New York: Basic Books.

America, R.F., Jr. (1977). *Developing the Afro-American economy*. Lexington, MA: Lexington Books.

Ando, F.H. (1986). An analysis of the formation and failure rates of minority-owned firms. *The Review of Black Political Economy, 15*, 51-71.

Ando, F.H. (1988). Capital issues and the minority-owned business. *The Review of Black Political Economy, 16*, 77-109.

Armstrong, O.K. (1974). Booker T. Washington—Apostle of good will. In H. Hawkins (Ed.), *Booker T. Washington and his critics: Black leadership in crisis* (pp. 3-9). Lexington, MA: D.C. Heath and Company.

Background and issues relating to the application of code section 1071 under the Federal Communications Commissions's tax certification program: Hearing before the Subcommittee on Oversight of the House Committee on Ways and Means, 104th Cong., 1st sess. (1995).

Bates, T. (1973a). *Black capitalism: A quantitative analysis*. New York: Preager.

Bates, T. (1973b). An econometric analysis of lending to black businessmen. *Review of Economics and Statistics, 55,* 272-283.

Bates, T. (1974). Employment potential of inner city black enterprise. *The Review of Black Political Economy, 5,* 59-67.

Bates, T. (1982). Effectiveness of the Small Business Administration in financing minority businesses. *The Review of Black Political Economy, 11,* 321-336.

Bates T. (1984-85). Urban economic transformation and minority business opportunities. *The Review of Black Political Economy,* 13, 21-35.

Bates, T. (1986). Characteristics of minorities who are entering self employment. *The Review of Black Political Economy, 15,* 31-49.

Bates, T. (1989). Small business viability in the urban ghetto milieu. *Journal of Regional Science, 29,* 625- 643.

Bates, T. (1990). Entrepreneur human capital inputs and small business longevity. *The Review of Economics and Statistics, 74,* 551-559.

Bates, T. (1993). *Banking on black enterprise: The potential of emerging firms for revitalizing urban economies.* Washington, DC: Joint Center for Political and Economic Development.

B.E. financial companies. (1995, June). *Black Enterprise, 25,* 163.

B.E. industrial/service 100. (1995, June). *Black Enterprise, 25,* 99-108.

B.E. insurance companies. (1995, June). *Black Enterprise, 25,* 165.

Bearse, P.J. (1986). An econometric analysis of black entrepreneurship. *The Review of Black Political Economy,* 15, 111-134.

Berndt, H.E. (1977). *New rulers in the ghetto: The community development corporation and urban poverty.* London: Greenwood Press.

Birch, D.L. (1987). *Job creation in America: How our smallest companies put the most people to work.* New York: The Free Press.

Blacks who left dead-end jobs to go it alone. (1984, February). *Business Week,* 104.

Blaustein, A.I., & Faux, G. (1972). *The star spangled hustle.* Garden City, NY: Doubleday & Company.

Boggs, J. (1971). The myth and irrationality of black capitalism. In R.W. Bailey (Ed.), *Black business enterprise* (pp. 150-158). New York: Basic Books.

Brimmer, A. (1971). Small business and economic development in the Negro community. In R.W. Bailey (Ed.), *Black business enterprise* (pp. 164-172). New York: Basic Books.

Brimmer, A. (1984). Long term economic growth and black employment opportunities. *The Review of Black Political Economy, 13*, 61-73.

Brimmer, A., & Terrell, H.S. (1971). The economic potential of black capitalism. *Public Policy, 19*, 289-307.

Broderick, F.L. (1974). The fight against Booker T. Washington. In H. Hawkins (Ed.), *Booker T. Washington and his critics: Black leadership in crisis* (pp. 67- 80). Lexington, MA: D.C. Heath and Company.

Brown, T. (1986, September 17). A freedom network takes shape. *The Philadelphia New Observer*, p. 2.

Bruno, A. (1996). *Affirmative action in the 104th Congress: Selected legislation* (Report No. IB95094). Washington, DC: Congressional Research Service, The Library of Congress.

Budget of the United States Government, Fiscal Year 1998. (1997). Washington, DC: U.S. Government Printing Office.

Butler, J.S. (1991). *Entrepreneurship and self-help among black Americans: A reconstruction of race and economics*. Albany, New York: State University of New York Press.

Butler, S.M. (1981, July 16). The Urban Jobs and Enterprise Zone Act of 1981 (S.1310, H.R. 3824). *The Heritage Foundation Issue Bulletin*, 1-16.

Center for Community Change. (1995, July 19). House Banking Committee votes to gut CRA. *CRA Watch, 2*, 1-7.

Chen, G.M., & Cole, J.A. (1988). The myths, facts, and theories of ethnic, small-scale enterprise financing. *The Review of Black Political Economy, 16*, 111-123.

Cole, J.A., & Reuben, L.J. (1986). Linkages between minority business characteristics and minority bank locations. *The Review of Black Political Economy, 15*, 73-92.

Coles, F., Jr. (1982). Notes on economic development and blacks. *The Review of Black Political Economy, 11*, 397-411.

Community Reinvestment Act, 12 U.S.C. § 2901 (1977).

Community Reinvestment Act Regulations, 12 C.F.R. Part 25, (1995).

Cross, T. (1969). *Black capitalism.* New York: Anthem.

Cruse, H. (1971). The black economy. In R.W. Bailey (Ed.), *Black business enterprise* (pp. 86-98). New York: Basic Books.

Daniels, B., Barbe, N., & Lirtzman, H. (1981). Small business and state economic development. In R. Friedman & W. Schweke (Eds.), *Expanding the opportunity to produce: Revitalizing the American economy through new enterprise development: A policy reader* (pp. 42-49). Washington, DC: Corporation for Enterprise Development.

Davidson, B. (1968). *Africa in history.* New York: Collier Books.

Dellinger, W. (1995, June 28). *Memorandum to General Counsels.* (Available from the U.S. Department of Justice, Office of Legal Counsel, Washington, DC 20530).

DeLorean, J.Z. (1969). The problem. In W.F. Haddad & G.D. Pugh (Eds.), *Black economic development* (pp. 7-20). Englewood NJ: Prentice-Hall.

Drake, St. C., & Cayton, H. (1971). Negro business: Myth and fact. In R. W. Bailey (Ed.), *Black business enterprise* (pp. 61-72). New York: Basic Books.

Du Bois, W.E.B. (1903). *The Negro church.* Atlanta: Atlanta University Press.

Du Bois, W.E.B. (1907). *Economic co-operation among Negro Americans.* Atlanta: Atlanta University Press.

Du Bois, W.E.B. (1940). *Dawn of dusk.* New York: Harcourt, Brace, and Company.

Du Bois, W.E.B. (1969). *The souls of black folk.* New York: New American Library.

Du Bois, W.E.B. (1971). *The Negro in business.* New York: AMS Press.

Economic report of the president, 1995. (1995). Washington, DC: U.S. Government Printing Office.

Economic report of the president, 1997. (1997). Washington, DC: U.S. Government Printing Office.

Eddy, M. (1993). *Minority and women-owned business programs of the federal government* (Report No. 93-331 GOV). Washington, DC: Congressional Research Service, The Library of Congress.

Edmond, A., Jr. (1988, June). Dealing at the speed of light. *Black Enterprise, 18,* 150-162.

Elliot, A.W. (1969). Black capitalism and the business community. In W.F. Haddad & G.D. Pugh (Eds.), *Black economic development* (pp. 74-84). Englewood Cliffs, NJ: Prentice Hall.

Farley, R. (1981). Poverty and enterprise: Towards the sixth stage of economic growth. *The Review of Black Political Economy, 11,* 229-250.

Fratoe, F.A. , Ph.D. (1994). *MBDA research and policy report—major recommendations from MBDA staff/sponsored research: An update.* Washington, DC: Minority Business Development Agency.

Fratoe, F.A., Ph.D. (1995). *Justification for the ongoing role of the Minority Business Development Agency.* Washington, DC: Minority Business Development Agency.

Frazier, E.F. (1971). Negro business: A social myth. In R.W. Bailey (Ed.), *Black business enterprise* (pp. 73-85). New York: Basic Books.

Garvey, A.J. (1967). *Philosophy and opinion of Marcus Garvey.* London: Frank Cass and Company.

Green, G., & Faux, G. (1969). The social utility of black enterprise. In W.F. Haddad & G.D. Pugh (Eds.), *Black economic development* (pp. 21-37). Englewood Cliffs, NJ: Prentice-Hall.

Green, M.F. (Ed.). (1989). *Minorities on campus: A handbook for enhancing diversity.* Washington, DC: American Council on Education.

Green, S., & Pryde, P. (1989). *Black entrepreneurship in America.* New Brunswick, NJ: Transaction Publishers.

Grown, C., & Bates, T. (1992). Commercial bank lending practices and the development of black-owned construction companies. *Journal of Urban Affairs, 14,* 25-41.

Handy, J., & Swinton, D.H. (1983). *The Determinants of the growth of black-owned businesses: A preliminary analysis.* Washington, DC: US Department of Commerce, Minority Business Development Agency.

Handy, J., & Swinton, D. H. (1984). The determinants of the rate of growth of black-owned businesses: A preliminary analysis. *The Review of Black Political Economy, 12,* 85-110.

Harlan, L.R. (1968). *Booker T. Washington in Perspective.* R. W. Smock (Ed.), Jackson: University Press of Mississippi.

Harrison, B. (1971). Economic development planning for urban slums. In R.W. Bailey (Ed.), *Black business enterprise* (pp.193-204). New York: Basic Books.

Harvard Law Review. (1971). Community development corporations: A new approach to the poverty problem. In R.W. Bailey (Ed.), *Black business enterprise* (pp.269- 289). New York: Basic Books.

Hawkins, H. (Ed.). (1974). *Booker T. Washington and his critics: Black leadership in crisis,* Lexington, MA: DC Heath and Company.

Hazen, D. (Ed.). (1992). *Inside the L.A. riots.* New York: Institute for Alternative Journalism.

Hill, R.B. (1981). *Economic policies and black progress: Myths and realities.* Washington, DC: National Urban League.

Innis, R. (1969). Separatist economics: A new social contract. In W. F. Haddad and G. D. Pugh (Eds.), *Black economic development* (pp. 50-59). Englewood Cliffs, NJ: Prentice-Hall.

Jaynes, G.D., & Williams, R.M., Jr. (Eds.).(1989). *A common destiny: Blacks and American society.* Washington, DC: National Academy Press.

Kalton, G. (1983). *Introduction to survey sampling.* Newbury, CA: Sage Publications.

Kelso, L.0., & Hetter, P. (1971). Equality of economic opportunity through capital ownership. In R.W. Bailey (Ed.), *Black business enterprise* (pp. 233-242). New York: Basic Books.

Kish, L. (1965). *Survey sampling.* New York: John Wiley and Sons.

Kotlowitz, Alex. (1988, February 26). Racial gulf: Blacks' hopes, raised by '68 Kerner report, are mainly unfulfilled. *The Wall Street Journal,* pp. A1, A9.

Lee, E.S., Forthofer, R.N., & Lorimer, R.J. (1989). *Analyzing complex survey data.* Newbury Park, CA: Sage Publications.

Lee, F.M. (1995, June 23). Memorandum: An analysis of the June 12, 1995, U.S. Supreme Court Decision in Adarand Constructors, Inc. v. Peña. (Available from the Minority Business Enterprise Legal Defense and Education Fund, 900 Second Street, N.E., #8, Washington, DC 20002)

Lee, R.F. (1973). *The setting for black business development.* Ithaca, NY: New York State School of Industrial and Labor Relations.

Levitan, S.A., & Miller, E. I.(1992). Enterprise zones are no solution for our blighted areas. *Challenge, 35,* 4-8.

Light, I. (1972). *Ethnic enterprise in America.* Berkeley: University of California Press.

Loury, G.C. (1981). Black economic progress: Reality and the illusion. *The Review of Black Political Economy,* 10, 355-379.

Loury, G.C. (1984). Internally directed action for black community development: the next frontier for "The Movement." *The Review of Black Political Economy,* 13, 31-46.

Mann, P.H. (1990). Nontraditional business education for black entrepreneurs: Observations from a successful program. *Journal of Small Business Management,* April, 30-36.

Marable, M. (1983). *How capitalism underdeveloped black America: Problems in race, political economy and society.* Boston: South End Press.

Markwalder, D. (1981). The potential for black business. *The Review of Black Political Economy, 11,* 303-314.

Marshall, W., & Schram, M. (1993). *Mandate for change.* Berkleybrook, NY: Progressive Policy Institute.

Mathews, B. (1971). The continuing debate: Washington vs. Du Bois. In R. W. Logan (Ed.), *W.E.B. Du Bois: A profile,* New York: Hill and Wang.

McClaughry, J. (1969). Black ownership and national politics. In W.F. Haddad & G.D. Pugh (Eds.), *Black economic development* (pp.38-49). Englewood Cliffs, NJ: Prentice-Hall.

McKersie, R. (1971). Vitalize black enterprise. In R.W. Bailey (Ed.), *Black business enterprise* (pp. 101-113). New York: Basic Books.

McLaurin, D.S. (1971). Ghetto economic development and industrialization plan (Ghediplan). In R.W. Bailey (Ed.), *Black business enterprise* (pp. 184-192). New York: Basic Books.

McLaurin, D.S., & Tyson, C.D. (1969). The Ghediplan for economic development. In W.F. Haddad & G.D. Pugh (Eds.), *Black economic development* (pp. 126-137). Englewood Cliffs, NJ: Prentice-Hall.

McNeish, P.F. (1969). Where does the money come from. In W.F. Haddad & G.D. Pugh (Eds.), *Black economic development* (pp. 85-97). Englewood Cliffs, NJ: Prentice-Hall.

Meier, A. (1971). The paradox of W.E.B. Du Bois. In R.W. Logan (Ed.), *W.E.B. Du Bois: A profile* (pp. 38-83). New York: Hill and Wang.

National Black Leadership Roundtable. (1982). *The black leadership family plan for the unity, survival, and progress of black people.* Washington, DC: Author.

National Center for Education Statistics. (1988, 1994). *Digest of education statistics.* Washington, DC: U.S. Government Printing Office.

Neter, J., Wasserman, W., & Kutner, M.H. (1989). *Applied linear regression models.* Homewood, IL: Irwin.

Nucci, A. (1992). *The characteristics of business owners database.* Washington, DC: U.S. Bureau of the Census.

Omnibus Budget Reconciliation Act of 1993, Pub. L. No. 103- 66, § 13301-13303 (1993).

Ong, P.M. (1982). Factors influencing the size of the black business community. *The Review of Black Political Economy, 11,* 313-319.

Papier, D., & Isaiah, J.P. (1987, September 23). More blacks create own firms, leave corporations. *The Washington Times,* pp. A1, B5.

Personal Responsibility and Work Opportunity Reconciliation Act, Pub. L. No. 104-193 (1996).

Puryear, A. N., & West, C. A. (1973). *Black enterprise.* New York: Anchor Books.

Randolph, L.B. (1988, December). Black students battle racism on college campuses. *Ebony, 44, 126-130.*

Regents of the University of California v. Bakke, U.S. 265 (1978).

Report of the National Advisory Commission on Civil Disorders. (1968). New York: Bantam Books.

Rudd, D.C. (1995, September). Lessons to learn. *Emerge,* 20- 23.

Samuels, H. (1969). Compensatory capitalism. In W.F. Haddad & G.D. Pugh (Eds.), *Black economic development* (pp. 60-73). Englewood Cliffs, NJ: Prentice-Hall.

Schuchter, A. (1971). Conjoining black revolution and private enterprise. In R.W. Bailey (Ed.), *Black business enterprise* (pp. 205-232). New York: Basic Books.

Schumpeter, J.A. (1949). *The theory of economic development: An inquiry into profits, capital, credits, interest, and the business cycle.* Cambridge, MA: Harvard University Press.

Scott, E.P., & Jensin, J. (1977). Accessibility to government resources for minority business development: A practicum. *The Review of Black Political Economy, 8,* 43-61.

Shapero, A. (1981). The role of entrepreneurship in economic development at the less-than-national level. In R.F. Friedman & W. Schweke (Eds.), *Expanding the opportunity to produce: Revitalizing the American economy through new enterprise development: A policy reader (pp. 25-35).* Washington, DC: Corporation for Enterprise Development.

Simms, M.C., & Burbridge, L.C. (1986). *Minority business formation and failure by industry and by location.* Washington, DC: United States Department of Commerce, Minority Business Development Agency.

Sinnette, E.D. (1989). *Arthur Alfonso Schomburg: Black bibliophile and collector.* Detroit: The New York Public library & Wayne State University Press.

Small Business Act, 15 U.S.C. 631 (1953).

Small Business Administration, Planning and Program Evaluation Division, Office of Planning Research and Data Management. (1977). *Evaluation of the SBA Small Business Investment Company Program: From inception in 1958 through March 1975.* Washington, DC: SBA.

Small Business Investment Act, 15 U.S.C. 661 (1958).

Smith, J.P. (1984, September). Race and human capital. *The American Economic Review,* 74, 685-698.

Smith, J.P., & Welch, F.R.(1986). *Closing the gap: Forty years of economic progress for blacks.* Santa Monica, CA: Rand.

Spratlen, T.H. (1973). The black consumer response to black business. *The Review of Black Political Economy, 4, 73-105.*

Statement of Eugene A. Ludwig, Comptroller of the Currency, Final Regulation on Community Reinvestment Act. (1995, April 19). (Press Release).

Statement of Senator Carol Moseley-Braun on H.R. 831. (1995, March 24).

Status of small business investment companies: Hearing before the Committee on Small Business, 104th Cong., 1st sess., (1995). (Testimony of Jim Wells).

Stephanopoulos, G., & Edley, C., Jr. (1995). *Affirmative action review: Report to the president*: Washington, DC: U.S. Government Printing Office

Stevens, R.L. (1984). Measuring minority business formation and failure. *The Review of Black Political Economy, 12,* 71-84.

Sturdivant, F.D., (1971). The limits of black capitalism. In R.W. Bailey (Ed.), *Black business enterprise* (pp. 114-123). New York: Basic Books.

Tabb, W. K. (1970). *The political economy of the black ghetto.* New York: W.W. Norton and Company.

Tabb, W.K. (1979). What happened to black business enterprise. *The Review of Black Political Economy, 9, 392-415.*

Tate, C. (1971). Brimmer and black capitalism: An analysis. In R.W. Bailey (Ed.), *Black business enterprise* (pp. 173-179). New York: Basic Books.

Thompson, G. L. (1995). High court refusal of Banneker appeal criticized: A "negative message" for African American youth? *Black Issues in Higher Education, 12,* 78-79.

Tiebout, C.M. (1962). *The community economic based study committee for economic development.* New York: The Committee for Economic Development.

Ulmer, A. (1971). Cooperatives and the poor people in the south. In R.W. Bailey (Ed.), Black business enterprise (pp. 243-250). New York: Basic Books.

U.S. Bureau of the Census. (1975). *Statistical abstract of the United States: 1975* (96th edition). Washington, DC: Author.

U.S. Bureau of the Census. (1981). *Statistical abstract of the United States: 1981* (102nd edition). Washington, DC: Author.

U.S. Bureau of the Census. (1989). *Statistical abstract of the United States: 1989* (109th edition). Washington, DC: Author.

U.S. Bureau of the Census.(1990). *1987 Economic censuses: Survey of minority-owned business enterprises, black.* Washington, DC: Author.

U.S. Bureau of the Census. (1992a). *1987 Economic censuses: Characteristics of business owners.* Washington, DC: Author.

U.S. Bureau of the Census. (1992b). *Statistical abstract of the United States: 1992* (112th edition). Washington, DC: Author.

U.S. Bureau of the Census. (1994). *Statistical abstract of the United States: 1994* (114th edition). Washington, DC: Author.

U.S. Bureau of the Census.(1996). *1992 Economic censuses: Survey of minority-owned business enterprises, black.* Washington, DC: Author.

U.S. Department of Education. (1994). *An invitation to your community: Building community partnerships for learning.* Washington, DC: Author.

U.S. Department of Health and Human Services, Administration for Children and Families, Office of Community Service. (1994). *Demonstration Partnership Program Projects: Micro business and self-employment: Summary of final evaluation findings from 1990.* Washington, DC: Author.

Vaughan, R.J., & Bearse, B. (1981). Federal economic development programs: A framework for design and evaluation. In R. Friedman & and W. Schweke (Eds.), *Expanding the opportunity to produce: Revitalizing the American economy through new enterprise development: A policy reader* (pp. 307-329). Washington, DC: Corporation for Enterprise Development.

Vesper, K.H. (1983). *Entrepreneurship and national policy.* Chicago: Walter E. Heller International Corporation.

Verrilli, D.B., Jr., Lepow, L.H., Del Duca, M.F., & Jenner & Block. (1994, October). *Brief Amicus Curiae of Minority Business Enterprise Legal Defense and Education Fund, Inc., National Minority Supplier Development Council, Inc., National Black Chamber of Commerce, Inc., & National Association of Minority Contractors: Adarand Constructors, Inc., v. Federico Peña, Secretary of Transportation, et al.* (Brief No.93-1941). Washington, DC: Wilson-Epes Printing.

Vincent, T.G. (1972). *Black power and the Garvey movement.* San Francisco: Ramparts Press.

Vobejda, B. (1989, July 28). Gains by blacks said to stagnate in last 20 years. *The Wall Street Journal*, pp. A1, A20.

Washington, B.T. (1907). *The Negro in business.* Boston: Hertel, Jenkins & Co.

Washington, B.T. (1909). *The Story of the Negro: The rise of the race from slavery.* New York: Negro University Press.

Wetzstein, C. (1987, October 14). Anxiety precedes payoff for cutting the corporate tie. *The Washington Times,* C3.

Wheeler, C. (1987). A black leader finds freedom colored green. *Tony Brown's Journal*, 1st Qtr. 28-29.

Williams, Adley & Company; Chemical Securities Inc., & State and Federal Associates, Inc. (1994). *Securitization for publicly funded business development portfolios: The practitioner's handbook.* Washington, DC: U.S. Department of Housing and Urban Development.

Woolf, A.G. (1986). Market structure and minority presence: Black-owned firms in manufacturing. *The Review of Black Political Economy, 14,* 79-89.

Wright, R.E. (1971). Toward controlled development of black America. In R.W. Bailey (Ed.), *Black business enterprise* (pp. 159-163). New York: Basic Books.

Yuskavage, R.E. (1993, November) Gross product by industry, 1988-91. *Survey of Current Business, 73,* 33-44.

Index

able-bodied adults, xvi
Adarand Constructors, Inc. v.
    Peña, 36, 104
AFDC. *See* Aid to
    Families with
    Dependent Children
affirmative action
    recent challenges to, xv,
        34-36, 98-99
African economic system. *See*
    economic development,
    African influence
African Methodist Episcopal
    Church, the. *See* church
African trading system, 6-7
Afro-American Baptist Church,
    the. *See* church
Aid to Families with Dependent
    Children, xv, 102
    See also public assistance
American Council on
    Education, 99
analyses, data
    bivariate, 55-56, 61, 111-13
    hypotheses, 55-57

analyses (*continued*)
    multivariate, 57-59, 61,
        69-78
    nonresponse, 59
    normweighting, 60
    univariate, 55, 61-69
    weighting, 59-60

Banks
    discrimination in lending, 42,
        44-45, 83
    history of African-American,
        11
    lending by African-American
        owned, 43
    and regional economic
        factors, 49
    and securitization, 91
Bates
    African-American business
        growth, 40
    comparison of results, 70, 74,
        89, 103
    financial capital and business
        survival, 44- 45, 83
    inner-city economic

inner-city economic
  development, 44
statistical model, 53-54, 56,
  69, 107-8
Benjamin Banneker
  Scholarship, 97
black capitalism, 22
black codes, 12
block grants, xv-xvi, 103
Brimmer, Andrew, 18-19
budget, White House, 97
Bureau of the Census, U.S.,
  xiii, 39, 53, 59
business
  cooperative, 11-12, 16
  consequences of ownership,
    21-22
  and economic development,
    xvii, 22, 89, 104 (*see
    also* Bates, inner-city
    economic development)
  and economic status, xiii
  entry, xv, 33, 42
  formation and failure rates,
    42-43, 46
  growth
    rate of, 31, 39-43
    variation in, 42-50
  history, African-American,
    xiii, 6-16
  legal impediments, 12-13, 17
  mentor and internship
    programs, 96
  number of firms, xv, 31-33,
    39, 43, 61, 89
    by industry, 46
business (*continued*)

  limited African-
    American,16-19, 31-34
  promotion of, 4, 21
  skill, 22, 42
  small, xiii, xv, 5, 24, 52,
    91-92, 102
  supply and demand, 42-43,
    49
  survival, xiii, xvii, 44-48, 53
    data analysis, 55-59, 61-87
    differences, 49-50
    statistical model, 54, 56-57
    (*see also* policy, public,
    recommendations)
  training, 22, 24, 101, 103
Butler, John Sibley, 6, 18-19

capital
  human, 26, 53
  financial, 43-45, 53
  start-up
    and business survival, xiii,
      44, 46, 52, 56-87
    definition, xiii, 54
    federal programs, 32-33,
      89-93
    and micro-enterprise, 103
    venture, 22, 28-29, 90, 93
capital, access to
  and limited business growth,
    17, 24-25, 29, 42, 45,
    103
  loans, 42-43
  and managerial experience,
    101
  See also debentures; loans
capital formation, 25

capital intensive
  human, 47, 52
  financial, 46-47, 52
capitalism, 22
Census Bureau. *See* Bureau of
    the Census, U.S.
Characteristics of Business
    Owners Survey (CBO),
    xiii, xvii, 43, 53, 59
Chi Square. *See* analyses, data,
    bivariate; multivariate
Church, African-American,
    8-9
Civil War, 17-18
Clinton, William, 35, 93, 95
college. *See* education
Committee on Small Business,
    House of
    Representatives, 33
community control. *See*
    self-determination
community development
    corporation (CDC),
    23-24
Community Development
    Financial Corporation
    (CDFI), 93
Community Reinvestment Act
  college funds, 99
  revised regulations, 45
  and start-up capital, 92-93
Community Self-Determination
    Act of 1968, 23-24
Congress
  legislation on business
      ownership, 21, 33-35
  policy debate, xv-xvi, 105

Congress on Racial Equality
    (CORE), 23
consumer purchasing power,
    15, 43, 49
cooperative business. *See*
    business, cooperative
cooperative ownership, 23
Corporation, Subchapter S, 5,
    52
credit, access to, 22, 28-29, 93
  and limited business growth,
      17-18, 22, 45

data
  analysis. *See* analyses, data
  descriptive, 55, 64
  sets, 55
  source, 51, 53
database, xiii, xvii-xviii, 53, 60,
    87
debentures, 23, 28-29
Department of Agriculture,
    U.S. (USDA), 26
Department of Commerce, 27,
    29
Department of Defense
    (DOD), 30
Department of Health
    and Human Services,
    U.S. (DHHS), 26 , 102
Department of Housing and
    Urban Development,
    U.S. (HUD), 26
Department of Transportation,
    U.S. (DOT), 30

Depression, the Great
    impact on business, 10-11,
        17-19
development, centers business,
    22
    See also Minority Business
        Development Centers
Direct Student Loan, 96
discrimination
    and economic status, 3
    within churches, 8
    in lending, 44-45 (*see also*
        banks; loans)
    limited business growth,
        16, 35
Douglass, Frederick, 11
Du Bois, William Edward
        Burghart, 6, 13-16

earnings gap, 4
economic development,
    xvi-xvi, 4-6
    African influence, 6-8
    via land ownership, 12
Economic Development
        Agency, 30
economic disparity. *See*
    economic status
Economic Opportunity Act of
    1964, Community
    Economic
    Development
    Amendment, Title VII,
    24
economic status, xv, xvi, 3, 4
economics, development, 25

education
    and business survival, 46, 50,
        54
    college xiii, 19, 31, 51
        completion rates, 47
        data analysis, 56-59, 61-87
        entry rates, 47
        financial assistance 96-97,
            99
        Historically Black Colleges
            and Universities
            (HBCUs), 97-98
        See also policy, public,
            recommendation, college
            education
    elementary and secondary,
        94-96
    high school dropout rates, 47
    laws prohibiting, 8-9, 17
    voucher system, 95-96
emerging fields. *See* industry,
        emerging fields
employment. *See* jobs
employment, state
    and business survival, 49, 54,
        103
    data analysis, 56, 61-66, 74-
        78, 85
Empowerment Zone. *See*
        enterprise zone
Enhanced Communities. *See*
        enterprise zone
enslavement
    and cooperative business, 11
    consequences of, 8, 16-17
    and transition to business,
        12-18

enterprise communities. *See* enterprise zone
enterprise zone, 25-27
entrepreneurship, *See* business
executive branch. *See* White House

federal. *See* government
Federal Deposit Insurance Corporation (FDIC), 22, 31
Federal National Mortgage Association (FNMA), 90-91
finance, insurance, and real estate (FIRE). *See* industry, FIRE
financing. *See* capital; debentures; loans
firm. *See* business
Food Stamp Program, xvi, 102
franchise, 22

ghetto. *See* inner-city
Goals 2000 Educate America Act, 94
See also education
government, federal
  downsize, xv
  sales to, 51 (*see also* procurement, government)
See also policy, public, recommendations
gross domestic product, 54-55 64, 67
gross national product, 39

homestead acts, 11
Hope Scholarship, the, 97
See also education, financial assistance
hypotheses. *See* analyses, hypotheses

income
  of churches, African-American, 8
  and equity capital, 42-43
  of franchises, 22
  of insurance companies, African American, 10
  levels, xv
  low, xv-xvi, 92-93, 95, 102-104
  median, 3, 49
  middle, xv, 92, 102, 104
  of secret societies, 9
Indian Bureau Development Centers, 29
industry
  concentration 35, 42, 49-50,
    data analysis, 55, 64, 68-69
  decline, 52, 64
  emerging fields, xvi, 40, 51, 89, 105
  finance, insurance, and real estate (FIRE), xiii, xvii, 47-48, 51-59, 89
    data analysis, 61-87
  manufacturing, xiii, xvii, 46, 51-56, 89
    data analysis, 61-87

industry (*continued*)
professional services, xiii,
    xvii, 47, 51-59, 89
    data analysis, 61-87
    wholesale, xiii, xvii, 46-47,
      51-56, 89
    data analysis, 61-87
inner-city, 22, 24-26, 44
insurance companies
    African-American, 10
    and securitization, 91
Internal Revenue Service (IRS)
    5, 52-53
Interned, 95
interquartile range. *See*
    analyses, univariate

Jim Crow laws, 12
jobs
    African-American, xv
    creation of, xvi, 5, 21,
      40, 104
    and enterprise zones, 26
    growth due to business, 43,
      46
    private sector, xv
    promotion, xv
    provided by African-
      American firms, 40-41
    public sector, xv
Job Training Partnership Act, 4
Johnson, Lyndon, 3

Kerner Commission, 3-4
King, Rodney, 4

legislation. *See* policy; public

lenders, 91-92
    See also banks
Lewis, Reginald, 40-41
loans
    college, 99
    Department of
      Transportation, 30
    "portfolio effect," 42
    from securitization, 91-92
    See also capital; debentures;
      Small Business
      Administration
Los Angeles, 4, 25

Managerial experience
    and business survival, xiii,
      43, 47-48
    data analysis, 56-59, 61-87
    provided by CDCs, 23-24
    See also policy, public,
      recommendations,
      managerial experience
manufacturing. *See* industry,
    manufacturing
market, capital, 91
marketplace
    access to, 26, 29
    and economic development,
      5
mean. *See* analyses, univariate
median. *See* analyses,
    univariate
methodology, 51-60
micro-enterprise, 93
    See also policy, public
      recommendations,
      micro-enterprise

Minority Business
 Development Agency
 (MBDA), 29-30, 99-100
Minority Business
 Development Centers
 (MBDC), 29, 101-102
Mode. *See* analyses, univariate
Models
 economic development,
  22-27
 statistical, 51, 53-54
  linear regression, 56
  logistic regression, xiii,
   xviii, 56-58
Morrill Act, 98
mutual benefit societies, 9-10

National Association for the
 Advancement of Colored
 People, 15
National Negro Insurance
 Association. *See*
 insurance companies
National Research Council of
 the National Academy of
 Sciences, 3
National Service Americorp, 96
Negro Business League, 13
New York City Benevolent
 Society. *See* mutual
 benefit society
Nixon, Richard, 23-29
nonminority-male business
 comparison with African-
 American, 49-53, 55
 data analysis, 64-87

Office of Small and
 Disadvantaged
 Businesses (OSDBU),
 29

Panic of 1873, 17
 See also Depression, the
  Great; recession
partnerships, 5, 52
Personal Responsibility and
 Work Opportunity Act,
 xv
Pell Grants, 96
Podberesky v. Kirwan, 97
policy, public
 assessment of, 31-33
 needed for African-America
  business, xv, 37, 89, 105
 recent action, 33-37, 105
 recommendations
  basis for, xiii, xviii, 4-5,
   105
  hours worked in business,
   102
  new firms, 100-102
  education, 93-100
  managerial experience,
   100-101
  micro-enterprise, 102
  start-up capital, 89-93
population, target, 51-53
poverty, xvi, 3-4
Presidential Management
 Internship Program, 100
procurement, government, 2,
 29-31
 See also affirmative action

professional services. *See*
    industry, professional
    services
Proposition 209, 98
public assistance, xvi
Public Works Act of 1977, the,
    30

recession, 3
  See also Depression, the
    Great; Panic of 1873
 reconstruction, 12
redlining, 45
Regents of University of
    California v. Bakke, 98
regional economic factors,
    49-50
 analysis of, 52, 54, 69, 85
regression analysis. *See*
    analyses; models,
    statistical
Report of the National Advisory
    Commission on Civil
    Disorders, 3
Research
  limitations of previous, xvii,
    45-49
  qualitative, xvii
  quantitative, xvii-xviii
  questions, 51
  See also analyses
riots, 3-4, 21

secret societies, 9
securitization, 90-92
segregation, 17-18
self-determination, 23-24

self-sufficiency
  and business, 19, 102-103,
    104
  economic, xvi, 13, 16, 19
set-aside, 33
  See also procurement,
    government
slavery. *See* enslavement
Small Business Act of 1953, 27
Small Business Administration
    (SBA)
  certification, 29
  loans and job creation, 40
  loan repayment, 41
  programs, 27-28, 30, 35-36,
    41, 89-90
Small Business Investment Act
    Amendments, 29
Small Business Investment Act,
    28-29
Small Business Investment
    Company Program
    (SBIC), 28-29, 90
sole proprietorship, 5, 52
Specialized Small Business
    Investment Company
    (SSBIC), 29, 32, 90, 101
standard deviation. *See* analyses
Standard Industrial
    Classification Code
    (SIC), 46, 51, 53
Standard Metropolitan
    Statistical Area (SMSA),
    42, 49
statistics. *See* analyses
Student Loan Guarantees, 96

Subcontracting Compensation
  Clause, 36
  See also procurement,
    government
Supreme Court, 33-36, 97-98
Survey of Minority-Owned
    Business Enterprises,
    39, 43

Tax
  base, xvi, 5
  credit, 22, 97
  deduction, 22, 97
  incentives
    black capitalism, 22-23
    and education, 97, 99
    and enterprise zones,
      26-27
    and Federal
      Communications
      Commission, 34
    and managerial experience,
      100
Technology Innovation
    Challenge Fund, 95
  See also education, financial
    assistance
Technology Literacy Challenge
    Fund, 95
Temporary Assistance to Needy
    Families, xv-xvi
Terrell, Henry, 18-19
Tuskegee Normal and
    Industrial Institute, 12

underdeveloped nation model,
    24-25, 44

unemployment, 3-4, 25, 40, 49,

variables, 53-58, 61-87, 89
  See also analyses
variance. *See* analyses
viability, business.
    See business, survival

Washington, Booker T., 12-13,
    15
Welfare Reform, xvi
White House. xv-xvi, 33, 35,
    97
wholesale. *See* industry,
    wholesale